# A-Z Colour Guide to

# DO IT YOURSELF

# A-Z Colour Guide to
# DO IT YOURSELF

## John Sanders

LANGHAM PRESS

## Important Note

Always remember that the conversion factors listed above are really designed only to help those of us brought up on the Imperial system of measurement to form a mental picture of the modern metric units. Few imperial/metric conversions (or vice versa) are 100 per cent accurate. It is, therefore, generally best to select one system of measurement at the start of a job and stick to it. Since most of the products and materials you will need are now sold in metric units, the metric system is the obvious choice.

Remember, too, that in many industries imperial/metric equivalents exist that are not exact conversions. For example, the metric equivalent of the old 1 cwt bag of cement is 50 kg, not 50.8 kg. Although the differences may be small, they soon add up, and unless you have allowed for them in your calculations, serious errors can occur – ten 50 kg bags of cement will leave you well over a stone short if you really need ten 1 cwt bags. Once again, it is therefore best to avoid conversions if possible. Put your shopping list together using the units in which the product is sold from the very start.

First published in 1983 by Langham Press,
Langham Park, Catteshall Lane,
Godalming, Surrey
in association with Octopus Books Limited,
59 Grosvenor Street, London W1

Printed in Hong Kong

# CONTENTS

**Acknowledgements**

The Publishers wish to thank the following individuals for their kind permission to reproduce the photographs in this book:

Steve Bicknell/Octopus Books, 66-67; John Cook/Octopus Books, 51, 55, 74; Simon de Courcy Wheeler/Octopus Books, 27, 47, 50, 62, 70-71, 75, 86, 87 above; Chris Linton/Octopus Books, 34 left, 35; Bill Mason, 34 right; Octopus Books, 110; Reg Perkes/Octopus Books, 94-95; David Prout/Octopus Books, 46, 59.

# GENERAL MAINTENANCE

## ARCHITRAVES

An architrave is a type of timber moulding used mainly to provide doors, windows, and so on with a decorative surround. It covers any gaps between the structural part of the frame and the wall.

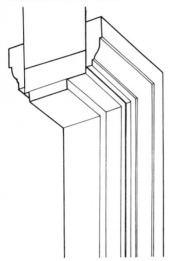

Normally made of softwood (though a large timber yard may be able to provide them in a hardwood suitable for varnishing), architraves come in a variety of styles.

## CASEMENT WINDOWS

The casement window or, more accurately, the casement sash window, is by far the most common design of window in current use. You will find versions made from softwood, hardwood, galvanized steel, aluminium, and even plastic. How-

ever, all are based on the following 'traditional' construction.

The simplest form comprises a 'structural' frame made up of two vertical jambs, a sill, and a head. This contains the casement sash itself – a subframe that carries the window pane – which may be fixed, or hinged if it is to be opened for ventilation. In the latter case, the hinges are usually fixed to a vertical stile, allowing the window to open rather like an ordinary door. However, small top-hinged versions, called fanlights, are also to be found. These are often used in the same outer frame, in combination with side-hinged and fixed casements to produce a composite casement sash window. Here, individual sashes are separated by vertical mullions and horizontal transoms.

To complete the assembly, the structural sill is fitted with separate inner and outer sills, the former known as a window board. There should also be built-in protection against rain penetration: a weather moulding or drip bead across the top, and a drip groove cut in the underside of the outer sill (to stop rain running back to the wall). Grooves may also be found in the mullions, transoms and frames to stop penetration by capillary action.

Whatever the details of the design, the timber casement's main weakness lies in the joints between the rails and stiles of the hinged sash. If these work loose, reinforce them

6

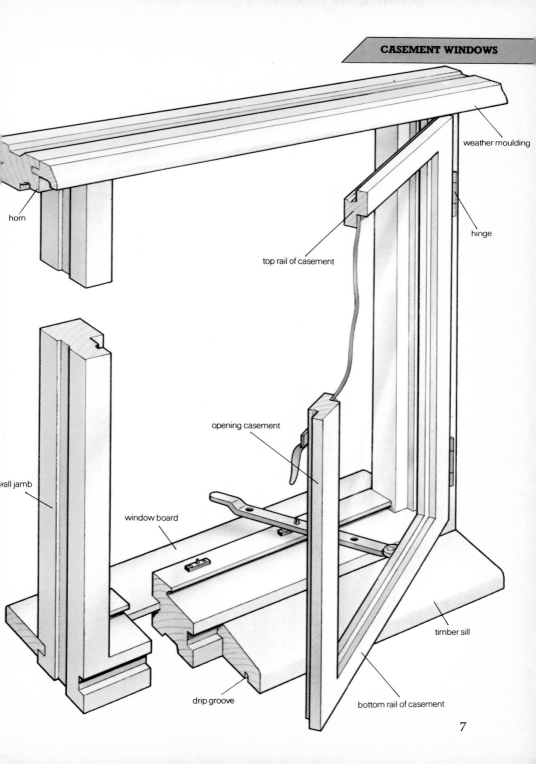

weather moulding

horn

hinge

top rail of casement

opening casement

wall jamb

window board

timber sill

drip groove

bottom rail of casement

7

with galvanized-steel angle repair irons, screwed into place and rebated into the timber. The latter allows them to be concealed with filler.

## CAVITY WALLS

A cavity wall (right) consists of two leaves of masonry separated by an air gap about 50 mm (2 in) wide. The masonry leaves are normally of brick, and they are linked at intervals by metal 'ties' which hold the wall together.

Used for the outer walls of houses, the cavity method of construction offers two main advantages. Firstly, the air gap prevents moisture passing from one side of the wall to the other, which should keep your home free of penetrating damp. Secondly, it offers some measure of insulation, slowing down the rate at which heat escapes from your home, and making the wall feel slightly warmer than if it were of solid masonry. In modern homes, the wall's insulation value is often enhanced by using aerated concrete blocks instead of bricks for the inner masonry leaf. A further improvement can be achieved by filling the cavity with an insulating material (see page 32).

To recognize a cavity wall, look at the way the bricks are arranged – the 'bonding'. Cavity walls are almost invariably 'stretcher bonded' (above).

## CEILINGS

Most ceilings are constructed of either plasterboard (a paper sandwich with a plaster filling) or lath and plaster (thin timber slats covered with plaster), fixed to timber joists which also support the floor above.

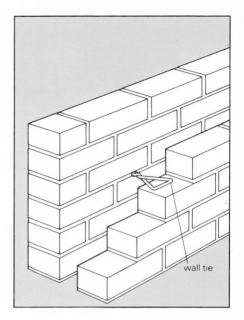

wall tie

Apart from filling cracks and small holes (see page 59), there is little you need do to them, with one important exception. Old age, dampness, and vibration can loosen the plaster covering of a lath and plaster ceiling, and, in this case, it is best to replace the whole lot with plasterboard.

Begin by pulling down every scrap of lath and plaster, using a crowbar or garden spade. This is a very messy job, so clear the room, close the door, and open the windows to disperse the dust. For your own protection, wear old clothes, safety goggles, and a face mask. Stand clear of sections that are about to fall. Remove any nails left in the joists.

You need to install additional timber supports ('noggins') for the edges of the plasterboard, and preservative-treated 50 mm$^2$ (2 in$^2$) timber

8

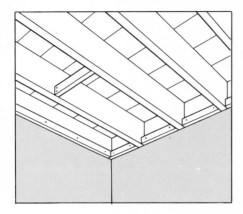

should be used. Cut this to fit between the joists, and fix it to the wall with galvanized screws driven into wall plugs. Extra 'noggins' are needed at intervals across the ceiling to support the plasterboard's edges (left), and these can be nailed in place.

Plasterboard comes in standard 2440 × 1220 mm (8 × 4 ft) sheets, so you will need help to hold each one up to the joists while you secure it with plasterboard nails driven in at approximate intervals of 150 mm (6 in).

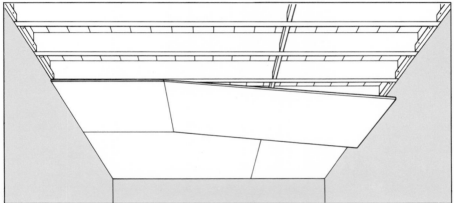

The important thing is to arrange the sheets so the joints are staggered brick-fashion (above). To cut the plasterboard to size, slice through the paper covering with a sharp knife and then use an ordinary fine-toothed saw.

Finally, prepare the plasterboard for redecoration. Cover both nail heads and joins with jointing scrim bedded in jointing compound (left). Apply more compound, feathering it out across the sheets, and finish by working a thin slurry over the ceiling.

9

## CORNICES & COVINGS

Very often there is confusion in the use of the terms cornices and covings, one being used to describe the other and vice versa. Cornices are horizontal decorative mouldings (traditionally of plaster, moulded *in situ*) along the tops of walls (top). They never touch the ceiling. Covings are mouldings that fill the angles between walls and ceiling (bottom).

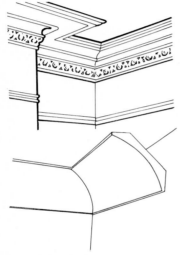

Repair minor damage to either moulding with filler. Failing that, remove damaged sections and replace them with matching prefabricated mouldings. Made of plaster or glass-fibre, these come in standard lengths, and may have mitred ends for a neat corner join. Expanded-polystyrene covings are also available, mainly for use with polystyrene ceiling tiles.

## DAMP

Before you can cure a damp problem, you must find out what's causing it; broadly speaking, there are five possibilities.

The first is rising damp – moisture soaked up from the soil by walls and floors. This is most common in older houses, modern ones having built-in defences: a damp-proof course (DPC), often of slate or roofing felt, in the walls, and a damp-proof membrane (DPM) of asphalt or plastic in solid floors. Even so, if these are faulty or are bypassed, rising damp can occur. Fortunately, it is easily cured (see page 36).

The second is penetrating damp: rain getting in through a part of your home that is supposed to keep it out. In simple cases, the fault may be a leaky roof, or gaps in and around a window frame. However, it can come in through the walls.

In cavity walls, penetrating damp should only occur if the cavity is 'bridged' by something able to carry moisture. Cavity-wall insulation is a possibility, but a more likely culprit is a deposit of mortar or other debris on the wall ties. In either case, seek expert advice. In solid walls, penetrating damp is only too common. General repairs, such as repointing brickwork and replacing defective rendering or cladding, should do the trick. If not, paint the wall with exterior paint or a waterproofing compound.

The third likely cause of dampness is faulty guttering, plumbing, etc. Repairing the fault will cure it.

Dampness may also be present in new building work. This is due to the fact that mortar, concrete, plaster, etc, have not dried out – it can take up to a year – so let nature take its

course. In the interim, choose cheap decorations that let moisture through (emulsion paints and wallpapers).

Finally, there is condensation. Most people put this down to the fact that warm air can carry more moisture than cold air, and so gives up some of its moisture as condensation if it meets a cold surface. What really matters, though, is how close the air is to saturation – its humidity. If it is very humid a tiny temperature drop can trigger condensation. The solution is to reduce the humidity.

You can remove water vapour before it does harm, with adequate ventilation. Don't be slow to open windows, and fit powered extractor fans in bathrooms and kitchens. Also, stop the air getting too cold. Set the heating to come on at regular intervals.

11

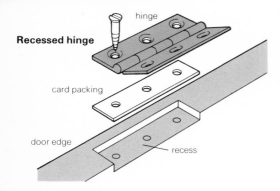

**Recessed hinge**

hinge

card packing

door edge

recess

## DOORS

Although doors are to be found in plastic and aluminium, the majority are still made from timber, using one of two construction methods.

A panelled door comprises a top, bottom, and centre (or lock) rail, joined to uprights called stiles. Additional horizontal and vertical members are inserted within this framework to create the panel design; the panels being infills of sheet timber or glass. This type of door is now available in a range of traditional and pseudo-period styles, often made in very attractive hardwoods.

For a flush door, the basic framework outlined above is filled with timber slats, or a sort of cardboard honeycomb, or a number of horizontal battens, and the door faced with plywood sheets.

When fitting a new door, make sure it fits squarely within the frame, leaving a 6 mm (¼ in) gap at the bottom, and a 3 mm (⅛ in) gap round the remaining sides. Saw off any stile extensions (these 'horns' are merely to protect the door's corners during transit) and hold the door in the opening, lifting it 6 mm (¼ in) clear

of the floor on timber packing. Then, use the frame as a guide to mark it out for trimming. The door must be held steady for this, so, if you are working alone, make up a suitable timber stand. Remove any waste with a long plane, remembering to work in towards the centre when tackling the end grain at the top and bottom (see page 115).

Having got a good fit, work out the hinge positions, and fix the hinges to the edge of the door (see page 26). On a flush door, the bottom hinge should be about 230 mm (9 in) from the bottom of the door; the top hinge 150 mm (6 in) from the top. If the door is heavy, add a third hinge half-way between the two. On a panelled door, the top and bottom hinges are located 25 mm (1 in) above and below the bottom and top rails respectively. Again, any third hinge fits midway between the two.

Cut matching hinge rebates in the door frame (prop the door in position to mark these out), and you are ready to hang the door. Once again, set it accurately within its opening, and mark the screw positions on the door frame by pushing a bradawl through the holes in the hinges. Fix the door in place with one screw per hinge, checking that it opens and closes smoothly. If it doesn't, the rebates are either too deep or too shallow, so cut them deeper or pack them out with thin card under the hinge leaves as required until you are satisfied (top left). Finally, drive home the remaining screws, and, having thoroughly sanded the surface of the door for decoration, fit the locks, handles, and so on (see pages 31-2).

## Hanging a door

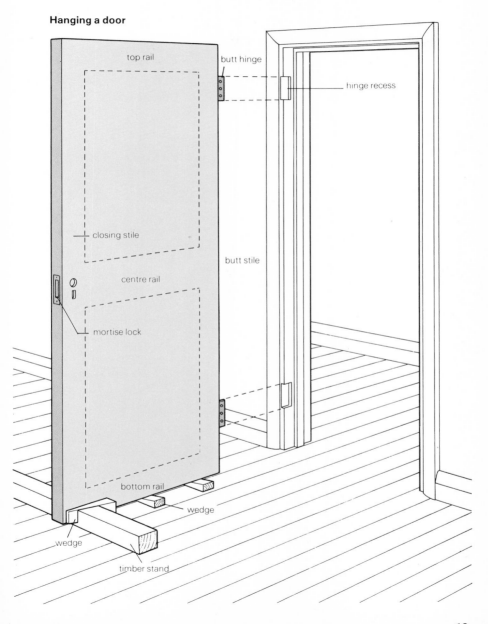

top rail

butt hinge

hinge recess

closing stile

butt stile

centre rail

mortise lock

bottom rail

wedge

wedge

timber stand

13

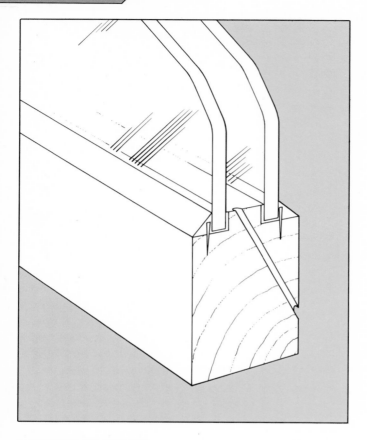

## DOUBLE GLAZING

Double glazing simply means fitting doors and windows with two panes of glass instead of one. This helps stop noise getting in, and heat getting out. However, it is not the extra glass that does the work – it's the air trapped between the panes. So, first choose the best size of air gap. To keep out noise it must be at least 50 mm (2 in); the best results come from gaps 100-200 mm (4-8 in) wide. For thermal insulation, a 19 mm (¾ in) gap is best.

The best way to fit double glazing is as a 'sealed unit'. Both panes go in the same frame, allowing the window to open normally. Whether or not this can be installed in an existing frame depends on the depth of the glazing rebate. Modern frames may accept factory-made units which you fit like a single pane of glass. If not, try modifying the frame to take separate panes (above), or improvise and cover the window with Cling-film.

The alternative is the 'secondary'

unit where the extra pane is given its own window frame (below). Professionally installed aluminium versions are best, but home-made units, and DIY plastic or aluminium kits are worth considering. Just be sure they don't interfere with ventilation.

Double glazing is certainly worth having in some rooms for comfort. Don't expect to make money out of fuel savings, though – you won't, unless using Clingfilm. Most systems need 10 to 20 years just to cover the cost of installation.

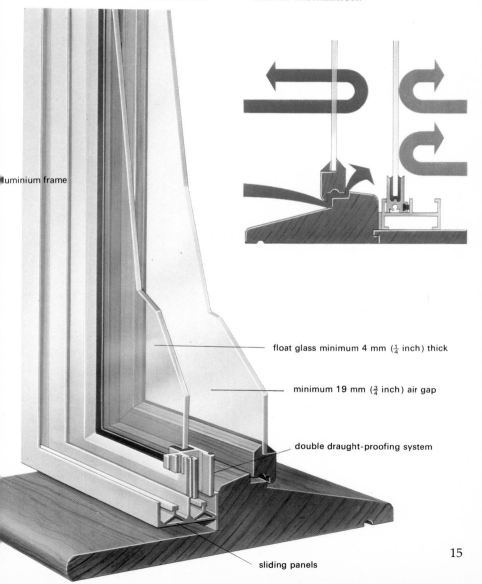

aluminium frame

float glass minimum 4 mm ($\frac{1}{4}$ inch) thick

minimum 19 mm ($\frac{3}{4}$ inch) air gap

double draught-proofing system

sliding panels

15

# DRAUGHTPROOFING

Draughts account for roughly 10 per cent of the heat lost from the average home; in an old house, it could be nearer 50 per cent. That means they cost you money in higher fuel bills, but there is no need because they can be substantially reduced by draught-proofing. This should pay for itself out of fuel savings in one or two years, making it one of the best investments going.

The illustrations below show some of the more common types of draughtproofing. Of these, the plastic foam strip is the least expensive,

the easiest to fit, and copes in most situations. However, the cheaper, less-dense versions are not very durable. In fact, they have been known to need replacement after a single season. Therefore, dense foam is a better long-term bet, but even this is unlikely to stand heavy wear and tear; use it only on rarely opened windows, loft trap-doors, and so on.

Elsewhere, go for a really tough draughtstrip. It may cost more, but it will last for years. Sprung-metal strips, or the plastic equivalent, are excellent. Small-scale versions of the plastic insert door threshold strip are

**Draught-excluders for doors**

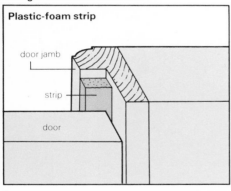

Plastic-foam strip
door jamb
strip
door

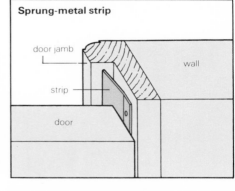

Sprung-metal strip
door jamb
wall
strip
door

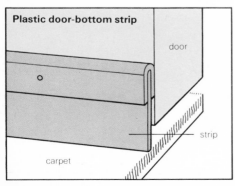

Plastic door-bottom strip
door
strip
carpet

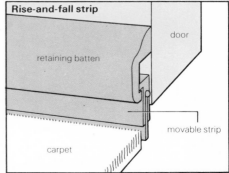

Rise-and-fall strip
door
retaining batten
movable strip
carpet

also worth a try. Sadly, none of the above work well on sliding sash windows. Special draughtproofing is available for these, but it is rarely very effective. Brush draughtstrips can be fairly useful.

There are quite a few draught-excluders to choose from when dealing with the gaps beneath doors. The simple rise-and-fall strips, bristle strips, plastic door strips, and plastic insert threshold strips are fine for internal doors, but for external doors, you need something more robust. An interlocking metal seal is best, backed up by an external weather strip. Alternatively, there are 'combination' strips with built-in weather seals, and/or heavy-duty rise-and-fall mechanisms.

Having said all that, it's a mistake to overdo draughtproofing. For all their faults, draughts play a useful role in ventilation, particularly in rooms containing fuel-burning appliances – gas and solid-fuel fires, etc. – so do not try to turn the house into an airtight box. Limit the draught-proofing to external doors and windows plus the loft's trap-door, and leave internal doors, unless leading to a room you hardly ever use.

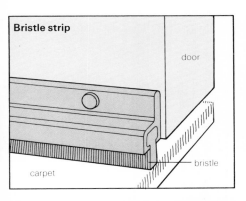

**Bristle strip**

door

bristle

carpet

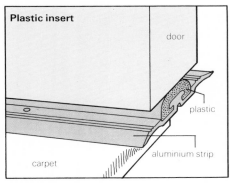

**Plastic insert**

door

plastic

aluminium strip

carpet

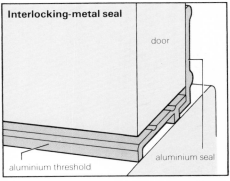

**Interlocking-metal seal**

door

aluminium seal

aluminium threshold

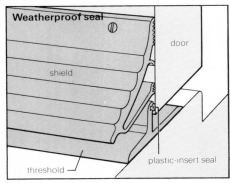

**Weatherproof seal**

door

shield

plastic-insert seal

threshold

## FIREPLACES

If you are one of the many now re-discovering the benefits of the open fire, it's worth knowing how to re-open a blocked-up fireplace.

If the opening is sealed with bricks or blocks, break these out with a club hammer and cold chisel. Often, though, the fireplace is just hidden by a sheet of plywood, hardboard, or plasterboard, nailed to a timber frame. In this case, the whole lot can be prised off with a crowbar. You may find that the old fireplace is virtually intact, needing only a new surround and superimposed hearth to get it working. However, it pays to carry out a detailed inspection.

Ensure the fireback, back hearth

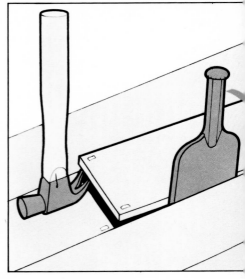

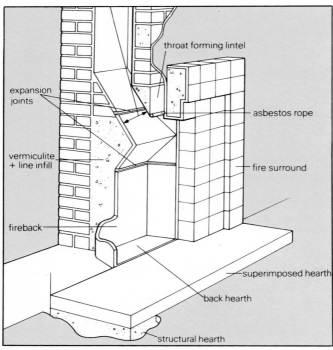

throat forming lintel

expansion joints

asbestos rope

vermiculite + line infill

fire surround

fireback

superimposed hearth

back hearth

structural hearth

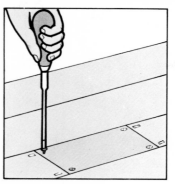

smoke leakage means the flue needs relining, and this, like clearing blockages, is best left to experts.

## FLOORBOARDS

Although very hardwearing, floorboards do occasionally need a little maintenance and repair.

When a board is damaged, rather than renew it completely, replace just the damaged section. Start by lifting the end nearest the damage. Take a stout, broad-bladed chisel (ideally, a special spade-shaped floorboard chisel) and tap this into the gap between the board and its neighbour. Then, use the chisel to lever the board upwards. As it begins to lift, insert a second chisel, or the claw end of a hammer, beneath the end to hold it while you adjust the first chisel to apply more leverage (above left). Eventually, the nails will loosen, and you can work your way along the board's length, levering against both edges and prising the rest of it free.

After lifting the board beyond the damaged section, support it on a long screwdriver, or something similar, balanced across the adjacent

and mortar flaunching are in good condition. If the fireback is damaged, you can make minor repairs with fireclay cement, but it is better to rebuild the fireplace from scratch – a job for an expert. If only the flaunching or hearth is damaged, repair this by chiselling out any loose material – be careful as flaunching is often soft anyway – and patching with a suitable mortar.

Finally, check the flue. Light a ball of newspaper in the grate and see that the smoke is drawn cleanly away. If it is not, this may be because the chimney was capped when the fireplace was sealed, or it may mean a blockage within the flue.

Next, burn an oily rag, or something similar that will produce a lot of smoke. Cover the fireplace to stop the smoke getting back into the room and then check for leaks along the entire length of the flue. Any trace of

boards while you saw through it above a joist. The damaged section can then be thrown away, and a new length of board fixed in place.

You may find that the damaged board is too weak to be levered, and, in this case, you must make a saw cut to free the damaged section. This should be flush with the edge of the first joist beyond the damage. Using a padsaw, begin the cut by inserting the saw blade into a hole bored previously with a brace and bit. Obviously, this leaves you without a joist to support the end of the board, so screw a length of 50 × 25 mm (2 × 1 in) timber to the side of the joist to provide a fixing point (page 19, centre).

There is one other snag. The whole of the foregoing assumes the boards are square-edged. Some, however, are interlocked with tongue-and-grooved joints. In this case, before you can lift the board – or even insert the chisel – you must saw through the tongue on each side of the board with a floorboard saw or tenon saw.

The other common problem is the squeaking floorboard. Sometimes, a cure can be effected by sprinkling French chalk into the gaps around the offending spot, but a more permanent solution is to refix the board with screws driven into the joists (page 19, right).

Finally, there may be gaps between the boards. The correct solution is to lift them all and to relay them closer together, though this is a lengthy and laborious operation. An easier method is simply to fill the gaps with papier-mâché, or timber fillets carefully planed to fit.

# FOUNDATIONS

Fortunately, foundations rarely give trouble, but you should be able to recognize this when you see it.

What you must look for are cracks, particularly in external walls; the most likely places for these are around window and door openings, and near the corners of the house where they tend to zig-zag upwards, following the mortar joins between bricks. You can ignore any that are less than, say, 3 mm (1/8 in) wide. These are almost certainly due to what is known as 'natural settlement'.

The cracks you have to worry about will be very wide, and, more importantly, will change size. They may get progressively wider, if due to general subsidence, or they may open and close. The latter is especially common on clay soils which shrink and swell according to how much moisture they contain. If you find such a crack, call in a Chartered Surveyor immediately to assess the situation, and check your house insurance. Correcting foundation faults can be cripplingly expensive.

Therefore, it is worth remembering that foundation problems can sometimes be avoided, simply by refraining from planting trees near the house. Tree roots not only exert direct pressure on the foundations, but also draw a great deal of water from the soil. Obviously, this could have very serious consequences if the subsoil's ability to support your house depends on its moisture content.

Whether you should chop down any existing trees will depend on how close they are. The usual rule of thumb is that no tree should be within 2 m (6 ft 6 in) of a house wall. Alternatively, you can try to establish the extent of a tree's root system, to see if it is getting too close for comfort. Roughly speaking, this corresponds to the spread of the tree's branches, but with many cases, it actually goes farther. Most garden trees are, after all, subject to pruning which both reduces the tree's spread, and encourages root growth.

It it seems likely that a tree's roots are getting under the house, then it will probably have to go. However, with large trees especially, it is well worth getting expert advice before you get out the axe. The reason is that the sudden removal of a tree, by allowing the subsoil's moisture content to return to 'normal', may well cause the ground to swell. This, in turn, can also damage the foundations.

## GLAZING

The first step, when repairing a broken window, is to choose the right type of glass for the job. For most situations that means float glass, which comes in several thicknesses; 3, 4, 5, 6 and 10 mm (approximately ⅛, 5⁄32, 3⁄16, ¼ and ⅜ in) are most common. The thickness you go for depends mainly on the pane's size and, to a lesser extent, on how likely it is to get broken. For most windows, 4 mm (5⁄32 in) glass is the norm, 3 mm (⅛ in) being suitable only for small or unusually sheltered windows. Large panes, however, may require a thickness in the 6-10 mm (¼-⅜ in) region, so ask your

supplier to advise you about this.

Glass 6 mm (¼ in) or more thick is also traditionally used in high-risk situations – for example, on glass doors, or where the window is low enough for someone to trip and accidentally fall through it. However, because even thick glass can break, producing viciously sharp fragments in the process, it is recommended that you use some sort of safety glass instead.

Toughened glass (also known as tempered glass) is by far the best. It is difficult to break, and, more importantly, if it should break, it shatters into relatively harmless crystals. Wired glass is another possibility. Wire mesh, embedded in the pane, holds it together when broken. Unfortunately, this does not make it any harder to break than ordinary glass. Finally, there is laminated glass – often used for car windscreens. Like toughened glass, this can take a lot of punishment before it will break, and when it does, it breaks safely. Even when smashed, it usually holds together, thus offering some protection against burglars. The snag is that it is very expensive, and is not widely available.

Whichever you choose, expect to have to order it. This is partly because safety glass is not widely stocked, and partly because both toughened and laminated glass are generally cut to size by the manufacturer, not by the glass merchant.

The precise technique for reglazing a window depends on what the window frame is made of, and the most common material is timber.

If the pane is cracked rather than

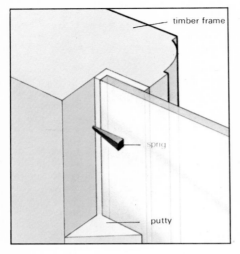

timber frame

sprig

putty

smashed, break it out with a hammer, having made sure there are no people or pets around to be hit by falling glass. Wearing thick gloves to protect your hands, remove every bit of broken glass. Any tiny fragments embedded in the putty should be tugged out with pincers or pliers.

Hack out the old putty, taking care not to damage the frame's rebate in the process. In the absence of a glazier's hacking knife, use an old, fairly blunt chisel. Remove any glazing sprigs – the small triangular nails (top left) that hold the glass in place – with pincers. With this done, sand the rebate to leave clean, bare wood. Brush on a thin coat of wood primer, and while this is drying, measure up and order the glass.

You need the internal dimensions of the rebate, and it is important that you measure them as accurately as possible. To allow for the fact that the frame may be out of square, measure both the width and height in two or three different places; take the smallest result in each case. Then deduct 3 mm (⅛ in) all round to obtain the size of the glass.

Before fitting the glass, line the rebate with putty. Given practice, you can squeeze the putty out between thumb and forefinger, pressing it into place at the same time. To begin with, though, you may find it easier to make putty 'sausages', roughly as thick as a finger, and then flatten them into place with your thumb.

Next, position the bottom edge of the pane on its bed of putty (top right) and press the glass into place with the palms of your hands, keeping to the edges. Never apply pressure to the unsupported centre of the pane or it may break. Check that it is centred within the frame, and continue pressing it inwards until it is within about 3 mm (⅛ in) of the back of the rebate. A certain amount of putty will ooze out behind it.

To secure the glass permanently in

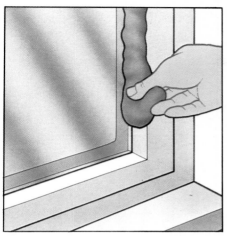

place you must 'peg' it with new glazing sprigs, but if these are not available panel pins with their heads snipped off are a good substitute. Drive these home with the pein of a hammer, sliding the head across the surface of the glass to reduce the risk of a poorly aimed blow sending you back to the glazier. If you find this difficult, try using the edge of a large, firmer chisel instead of a hammer. You need at least two sprigs per side, positioned 50-75 mm (2-3 in) from the corners, with further sprigs set roughly 300 mm (12 in) apart in between.

Finally, apply more putty round the rebate to cover the edge of the glass (above) and heads of the sprigs, using a putty knife to smooth it into a neat triangular fillet with mitred corners (above right). Wetting the knife blade will make this easier. Trim off the putty that oozed out behind the pane, and leave the window for about 14 days to allow the putty

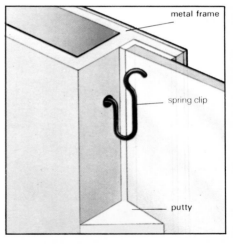

metal frame

spring clip

putty

to harden before applying primer, undercoat, and a couple of finish coats of gloss paint. Allow the final coat of gloss to overlap the glass by about 3 mm (⅛ in) to provide a weatherproof seal.

With galvanized steel windows the reglazing procedure is only slightly different. The old glass will have been secured by spring clips (over-leaf) rather than sprigs, and these should be kept for reuse with the new pane. Also, you must be sure to use a putty that is suitable for use on metal frames. The linseed-oil based putty for use on wooden windows will not work.

Last, but not least, there are modern aluminium and plastic windows. Here, the means of retaining the glass will vary from one make to another, but the most common method is a rubber gasket. Many makers prefer to reglaze the window for you, and this is not a bad idea where sealed-unit double glazing is concerned.

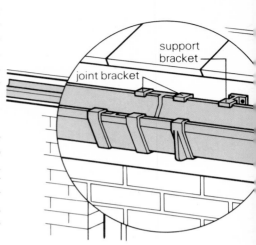

## GUTTERING

It is simple to replace defective cast-iron guttering. Rust will force its removal sooner or later, and doing it sooner will save you work in the long run.

The most popular replacement is made from plastic: unplasticized polyvinyl chloride (UPVC). It is available in a range of standard profiles and in several sizes. Its main advantages, though, are that it is fairly inexpensive, and that you can install it yourself. You merely buy the necessary separate components – straight lengths of gutter and downpipe, bends, hopper heads, and so on – and join them together *in situ*. Normally, this involves little more than pushing parts together, and snapping on retaining clips.

The alternative is aluminium sheet, formed into guttering on site by special machines. In terms of materials, it costs about the same

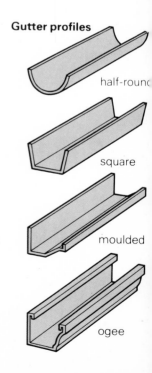

**Gutter profiles**

half-round

square

moulded

ogee

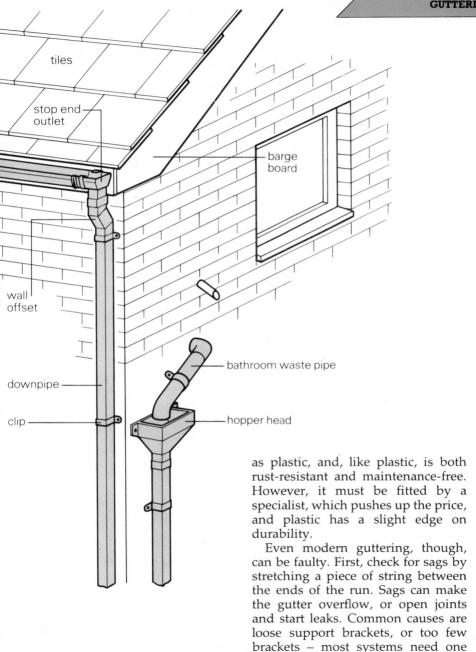

tiles

stop end outlet

barge board

wall offset

bathroom waste pipe

downpipe

clip

hopper head

as plastic, and, like plastic, is both rust-resistant and maintenance-free. However, it must be fitted by a specialist, which pushes up the price, and plastic has a slight edge on durability.

Even modern guttering, though, can be faulty. First, check for sags by stretching a piece of string between the ends of the run. Sags can make the gutter overflow, or open joints and start leaks. Common causes are loose support brackets, or too few brackets – most systems need one

**Butt hinges**

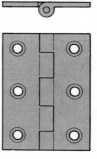

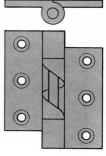

Simple butt

Rising butt

every 2 m (6 ft 6 in) or so. While you are about it, make sure the guttering has the correct fall, that is a downwards slope to a downpipe. Without it, overflows may occur in heavy rain. For every 1.8 m (6 ft) of gutter length, the downpipe end should be 3 mm (⅛ in) lower than the upstream end. Finally, replace any rubber seals in leaking joints.

Any further trouble will probably indicate the need for cleaning. Brush any debris into piles, and scoop it into a bucket for disposal. Wear rubber gloves, and temporarily plug downpipes with rag wads to stop bits falling in and causing another blockage. Then, having removed all rag plugs, flush out the system with clean water. As well as removing any remaining dirt, this tests the downpipes. If these are blocked, dismantle them and clean them out at ground level by pushing a rag wad through with a long, flexible cane. Finally, save any further problems by keeping the gutter clear. Clean it out at the end of the autumn to remove leaves.

## HINGES

Hinges come in a great many shapes, sizes, materials and designs, but, generally, only two are used on domestic doors – the butt and the rising butt (above). The latter lifts the door as it opens to clear carpets. Of the two, the simple butt is most common, and it is very easy to fit.

To mark out the hinge rebate, lay the hinge on the edge of the door and draw round it in pencil (top left). Go over the lines with a sharp craft knife, squaring up the outline with a try square (top right). The waste timber can be removed with a chisel. Cut round the outline and then chop the waste into manageable chunks, working first one way (centre left), then the other (centre right); clean out the rebate from the side (bottom left). Try the hinge for size, and continue until it sits flush with the surrounding timber. Finally, screw the hinge into place, using countersunk woodscrews (bottom right).

Rising butts are fitted in the same way, but the door needs some modification so that it clears the top of the door frame when opened. Mark the

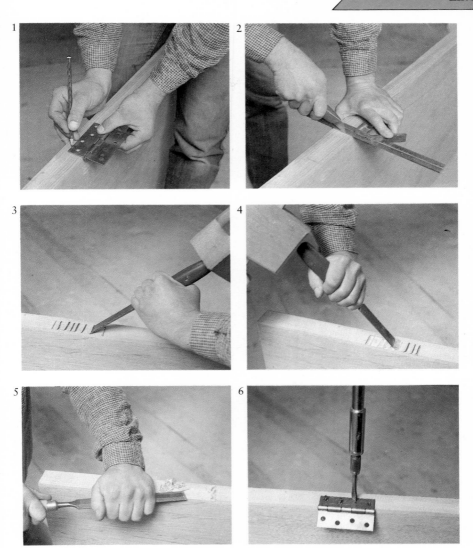

depth of the stop bead – the part of the door frame that stops the door swinging both ways – on the corner of the door between the hinge edge and the face that contacts the door frame. From this point, draw one line to the hinge edge's rear top corner, and another to a point midway along the top of the door face. Join these last two points with a line across the top of the door; plane off the resulting triangular fillet of waste.

**Solid-wall insulation**

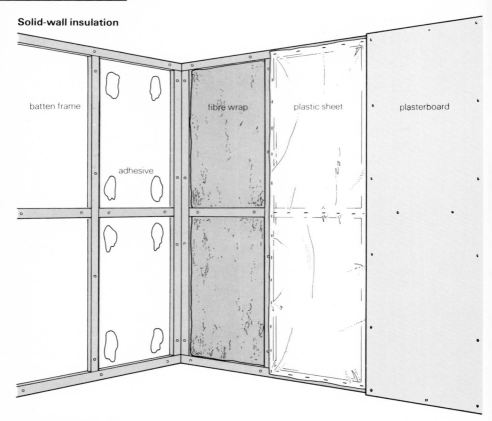

batten frame

adhesive

fibre wrap

plastic sheet

plasterboard

## INSULATION

With energy costing what it does these days, few of us can afford to waste it. Yet, unless your home is adequately insulated, waste it you will. Undoubtedly, draughtproofing and loft insulation offer the best value for money, and these, together with double glazing, are discussed under their appropriate headings. However, walls, floors and flat roofs also need attention.

The simplest way to insulate a cavity wall is to fill the air gap with insulating material – normally foam

plastic, mineral fibre or polystyrene beads. This must be done by a reputable specialist, and can be expensive, but with walls accounting for about 35 per cent of the heat lost from the average home, your investment should show a profit after about five years. Solid walls can also be professionally insulated by lining the outside with polystyrene slabs, covered by a special rendering. This, though, isn't such a good investment. You would do better to insulate solid walls yourself.

Begin by removing the skirting

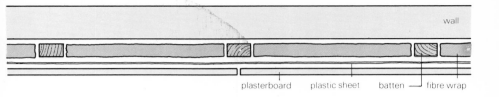

plasterboard    plastic sheet    batten ⎯ fibre wrap

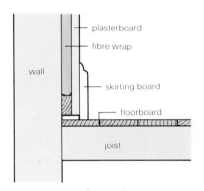

plasterboard

fibre wrap

wall

skirting board

floorboard

joist

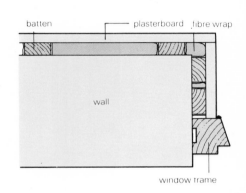

batten      plasterboard   fibre wrap

wall

window frame

boards, etc, and cover the wall with a framework of 50 × 25 mm (2 × 1 in) timber battens – use thicker timber for more insulation. Place glassfibre blanket, or expanded polystyrene, between these, cover with a sheet of heavy-gauge polythene to stop condensation forming within the insulation, and then line the wall with plasterboard (above left and above). Finally, replace the skirting boards and other fittings.

Floors are harder to insulate. If solid, cover them with dense polystyrene foam topped by chipboard or a mortar screed. If of suspended timber construction, staple paper-wrapped glassfibre blanket between the joists under the floorboards (below). Both involve a lot of upheaval, and so are really worth trying only in extreme cases.

In the case of flat roofs, if the roof or ceiling beneath it are being replaced, insulate in the same way as a suspended timber floor. Otherwise, consider fitting a false ceiling – plasterboard suspended below the true ceiling on a stout timber framework – with insulation above.

**Suspended-floor insulation**    floorboards      joists   paper-wrapped fibre wadding    staples

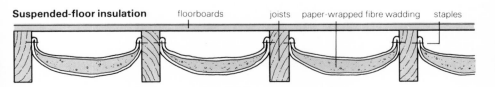

29

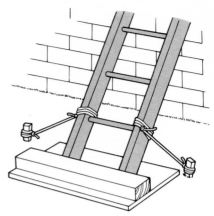

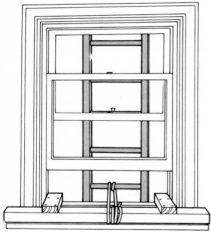

## LADDER SAFETY

If you carry out regular work around the house, eventually you will find the need for a ladder or a pair of steps, and it is vital you use them safely. There are two very important rules: don't use ladders or steps unless they are in excellent condition, and, if heights worry you, don't go any higher than is comfortable.

More specifically, ensure that the ladder is stable. Never rest the top against gutters, windows, or anything that might give way. If you must work with the ladder at a window position, tie a length of stout timber to the top to transfer the load to the walls on either side of the window opening (above left). Where possible, tie the top of the ladder to a batten spanning the inside of a window frame (left).

The foot of the ladder must also be secure, resting on a firm, level surface. On concrete, unless the ladder has rubber 'safety feet', stand it on sacking to stop it slipping. On soft earth, support it on a board with a batten to brace its feet, and tie it to stakes (above).

To improve stability further, put the ladder up at the correct angle. The distance between the foot of the ladder and the base of the wall should be equal to a quarter of the height to which the ladder reaches. Take care not to lean out too far to one side.

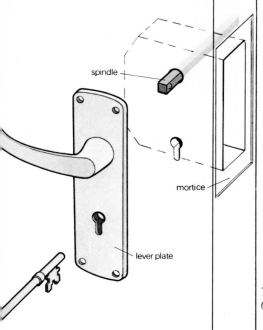

spindle

mortice

lever plate

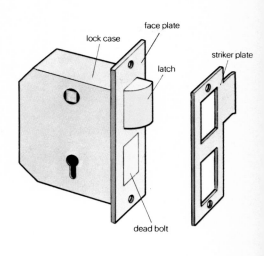

lock case

face plate

latch

striker plate

dead bolt

*Typical locks on domestic premises: mortice (above), cylinder (below).*

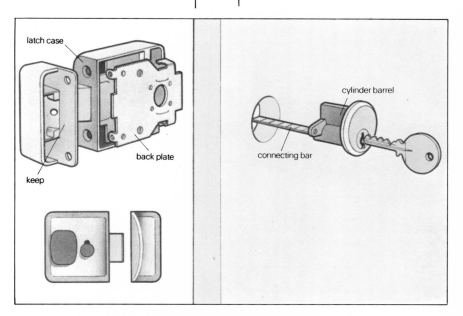

latch case

keep

back plate

cylinder barrel

connecting bar

31

## LOCKS & HOME SECURITY

A look at the crime statistics will tell you that, with burglaries on the increase, good locks are important. But where will they be of most use, and how do you choose the best locks for the job? The answers lie in a sound 'home security strategy' that will make your home secure, without making it an impossibly uncomfortable fortress.

All external doors need protection. Fit each with at least a couple of bolts – use a lockable type such as a mortice bolt if they can be reached through cat doors, broken glass and so on – and preferably a mortice lock. The door by which you normally leave your home should also have a good-quality cylinder lock. If its handle can be reached by breaking any glass, make sure it can be immobilized with a key. The small locking 'snib' provided on many models is not enough. A lock with a 'double throw', which shoots the bolt farther into the door frame, is also worthwhile as it will stop the bolt being slid back by, say, a credit card inserted between door and frame. Lastly, if the hinges are exposed, fit hinge bolts. These hold the door in place, even if the hinges are destroyed.

Sliding patio doors are more difficult to protect. Firstly, ensure they are of good quality, or it may be possible to lever them from their frame. Fit them either with a special patio door lock, or a lock fitted with a hook bolt. This will prevent them being slid open by force.

You should protect opening windows at ground floor level and any on upper floors that can be reached by climbing drainpipes, etc. If you don't need a window for ventilation, screw it to its frame using woodscrews or, better still, security 'dual screws' – the latter can be withdrawn with a key if you decide to open the window. Casement windows used for ventilation need two kinds of lock: a locking cockspur handle (or mini mortice bolts) to hold them shut; and a stay lock to hold them partially open. Locks similar to patio door locks are available to do both jobs on sliding sash windows.

It is unlikely that a thief will smash a window and climb in, unless the window is small, or positioned in such a way that the break-in cannot be seen or heard. However, if you are worried about this possibility, put up bars or a security grille.

## LOFT INSULATION

With about a quarter of the heat lost from your home going through the roof, loft insulation is very worthwhile, paying for itself within two years in most cases. The simplest method is to insulate the loft floor, preferably between the joists so you can use the loft space for storage, and there are two types of insulation you can use: blanket and loose-fill.

Insulation blanket is made from glassfibre. It comes in rolls of various widths (to fit over or between the joists), and in a choice of thicknesses, 100 mm (4 in) now being considered best. Laying it is simple, just unroll it, and cut it to size. Many people find that the glassfibre irritates their skin and lungs, so wear a face mask, old clothes and gloves. When you have finished, throw the clothes away and wash the skin thoroughly.

Loose-fill is kinder, and easier to lay in awkward corners, or where the joists are spaced unevenly. Whether granulated mineral fibre, or polystyrene beads, you pour it on to the floor and scrape it level with a wooden board. It, too, has its drawbacks. Strong draughts can blow it into drifts, exposing part of the loft floor. What's more, it isn't as efficient as the glassfibre blanket, which means you need a layer about 125 mm (5 in) thick. As a result, the joists will be covered.

There are just two other things to watch, whichever form of insulation you choose. Firstly, prevent condensation in the loft. Leave the eaves clear to provide ventilation, and lay plastic sheeting under the insulation to stop moisture-laden air filtering up from below. Secondly, the loft will be colder after insulation, so plumbing needs extra protection. Lag all pipes and tanks, leaving the loft floor beneath tanks uninsulated so that warmth seeps up from below to prevent them from freezing.

## POINTING

There are two ways to neaten the joins between bricks: you can shape the mortar used to bond the bricks before it sets – 'jointing' – or you can rake it out and tidy up, when the wall is finished, by adding fresh mortar and shaping that. The latter is called 'pointing'. Unfortunately, mortar isn't very weather-resistant. In time, it crumbles and cracks, making it easier for rain to get into the wall to weaken the mortar still further, damage the bricks, and cause penetrating

damp. Therefore, a speedy repair is important. This is called 'repointing'.

Remove the old pointing with a cold chisel and club hammer. Take care not to damage the bricks, and avoid cutting deeper than about 10 mm (⅜ in). Next, press fresh mortar firmly between bricks with a trowel until proud of the surrounding brickwork.

You can now shape the pointing, and there are three methods in common use (overleaf). *Flush pointing* is achieved by scraping off excess mortar with a piece of scrap board. *Profiled* (or *pail handle) pointing* is produced by pressing a dowel into the soft mortar. Tackle vertical joins first, then finish with the horizontals. Finally, there is *weather-struck pointing*. Again, tackle vertical joins first, using a trowel to press the mortar into a triangular fillet against the right-hand brick (top left, page 34). Having done that, run the trowel along the horizontal joins, with a straight batten as a guide, to form a fillet against the bricks below (top right, page 34).

## RENDERING

If you think of rendering as a mortar overcoat applied to walls to fend off the rain, you can see why it must be kept in good repair.

Rake out any cracks and fill them in the same way as cracks in plaster. The only difference is that you use mortar as the filler.

Blistering – rendering lifting from the wall – is more serious. Gently tap the wall, listening for a hollow sound which will indicate where the blistering has occurred. Draw round the

*Re-pointing brickwork.*

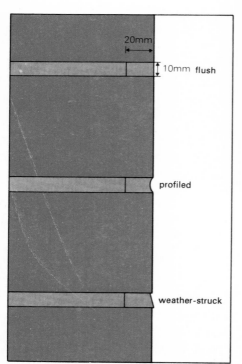

20mm

10mm flush

profiled

weather-struck

blister in chalk. Chop out the faulty rendering with a club hammer and cold chisel, starting in the centre and working out towards the edge. Brush off loose debris, wet the wall and apply a fresh coat of mortar with a wooden float (top left, opposite). Fill the hole to within about 12 mm (½ in) of the surface of the surrounding rendering. Allow this mortar to harden slightly. Then, with the edge of

the float, cross-hatch the mortar with scratches (top right) to key in the finishing coat.

Once fully dry, apply the finishing coat, leaving this proud of the original rendering. Saw off the excess with the edge of a straight batten (bottom left) and smooth off the surface with the float's face (bottom right).

Finally, having allowed the mortar to dry out for two to three months, paint the entire wall to disguise the repair.

To match roughcast rendering and pebble dash, simply mix fine aggregate into the finishing coat. Then, again, paint the entire wall.

Remember, though, that repairs are of limited value. If the damage is extensive, the wall should be re-rendered from scratch.

**Replacing a damaged tile**

**Replacing a damaged ridge tile**

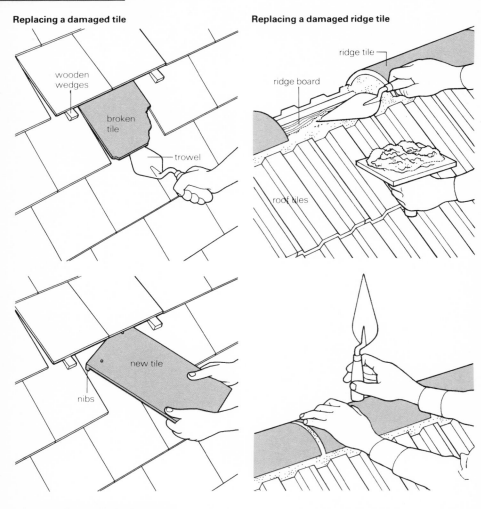

## RISING DAMP CURES

There are a number of cures for rising damp in walls, the most durable being to cut a slot in the masonry, just above ground level, and insert a physical barrier such as slate, zinc sheeting, or a plastic envelope filled with plastic foam. This is a specialist job and is expensive.

The usual alternative is to waterproof one or two courses of brickwork by saturating them with a waterproofing chemical (usually silicon based), which is injected under pressure through holes drilled deep into the masonry. This, too, is normally done by a specialist, but the necessary chemicals can be bought

36

**Replacing a damaged slate**

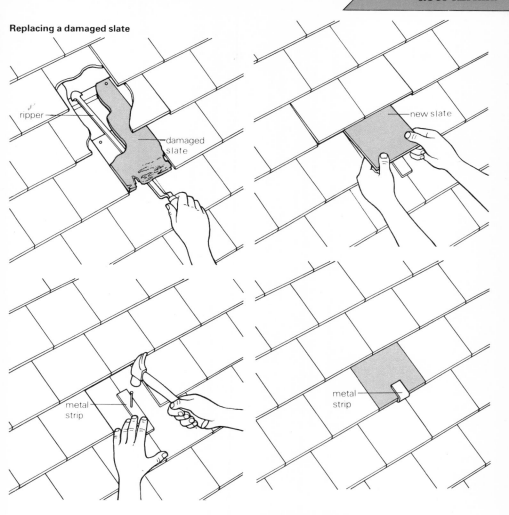

ripper

damaged slate

new slate

metal strip

metal strip

and the injection equipment hired from good tool-hire shops, allowing you to tackle the work yourself. In this case, follow the instructions.

When you have finished, fill the holes with mortar, and conceal them behind a rendered 'plinth' separated from the wall by a bitumen-emulsion damp-proof membrane.

## ROOF REPAIRS

A faulty roof is more than just an annoying destroyer of your home's decorations. If left unattended, it can quickly lead to serious faults in ceilings, walls, and structural timbers – all of which can be extremely expensive to put right.

The most likely cause of a leak is a

loose or damaged tile or slate. If the roof's underside isn't hidden by boards and felt, you can probably locate this from inside the loft. If not, check the outside from ground level, using a pair of binoculars.

To replace an old slate (see page 37), you need a tool called a slate ripper, which can be hired. Slide this beneath the slate, hook it around each of the fixing nails, and jerk it back sharply to cut through them and allow the slate's removal. A strip of soft metal such as lead or zinc (it's actually called a tingle) is then positioned in the gap and nailed into place. All that remains is to slide in the new slate, taking care not to weaken the fixings of surrounding slates in the process, and to bend the tingle into a flattened hook around its bottom edge to stop it sliding out again.

Tiles are easier to deal with because they are usually just hooked over the roof's horizontal timber 'purlins'; they have protruding 'nibs' for the purpose. Lift a couple of tiles in the row above and wedge them clear of the tile to be removed (see page 36). You should be able to lift this clear and hook on the new tile. If it won't come free easily, it has probably been nailed into place like a slate, so use a slate ripper to free it. There is no need to secure the new tile with a tingle, however; simply hanging it from the purlin, as already described, is quite sufficient.

Ridge tiles and ridge slates – those along the apex of the roof – can also come adrift as the mortar holding them in place weakens with age. Lift off the loose section and carefully

scrape off any mortar still clinging to it, before using a club hammer and bolster chisel to clean off the remains of the mortar bed on the roof (see page 36). Replace this with a thick bed of fresh mortar, press the old ridge tile or slate back into place, and finish off by pointing the joins around it.

You can see from this that roofing work is not technically difficult. However, it can be dangerous, so do take care. You will need a ladder long enough to reach at least 1 m (3 ft 3 in) above the eaves, and this should be fitted with a stay to stop it resting on the guttering. It should also be secured as firmly as possible at top and bottom (see page 30). To reach the damaged section of the roof, use a roof ladder – the sort fitted with wheels that allow you to push it up the roof slope and hook it over the ridge. Haul this up on a rope once you reach the roof; don't try to carry it up with you. Once on the roof, stay on the ladder. You may have seen professionals scampering about at will, but they know a slippery patch when they see one – you don't.

## SASH WINDOWS

The sash window – more correctly called the sliding sash or double hung window, because all windows have sashes – is normally found in older properties. The main reason for this is that, while the design does offer better control over ventilation than most, it is expensive to make, difficult to maintain, and a little too draughty for the taste of modern architects.

The glass is carried in upper and

lower frames, or sashes, each consisting of a top and bottom rail with a vertical stile at each side. Often, additional vertical and horizontal members are inserted in the frame to break up the window area into a number of smaller panes or 'lights'. The important thing about this design, though, is the way the sashes open; they slide vertically past each other, and can be held in almost any position by means of metal

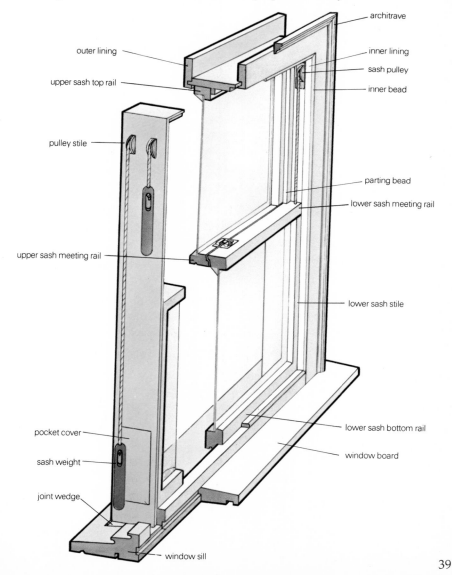

architrave
outer lining
inner lining
sash pulley
upper sash top rail
inner bead
pulley stile
parting bead
lower sash meeting rail
upper sash meeting rail
lower sash stile
pocket cover
lower sash bottom rail
sash weight
window board
joint wedge
window sill

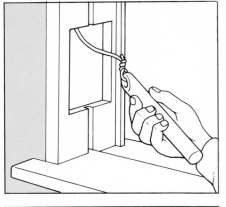
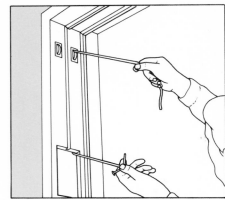
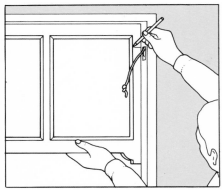
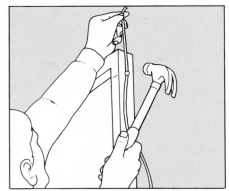

counterbalance weights.

These weights travel up and down inside a hollow window frame, being connected to the sashes by cords which run over pulleys set in the frame. The two side 'pulley stiles' are linked at the top by a crossmember called the yoke. The assembly sits within the opening on the usual window sill/window board construction, separated from the masonry by an inner and outer lining. Any gaps are covered by an architrave.

Lengths of beading are fixed to the pulley stiles to form vertical guide channels for the sashes. Normally, there will be a parting bead, separating the two sashes, and an inner, or staff, bead preventing the inner sash flapping back into the room. On the outside of the window, the staff bead's role is taken by the outer lining which should protrude beyond the pulley stiles and yoke. Finally, inserts, called pocket covers, are set into holes (pockets) cut into each pulley stile near the bottom, and they provide access to the sash weights for repairs.

Given the age of most sliding sash

windows, and their complexity, it is hardly surprising that things frequently go wrong with them. The most likely fault is a broken sash cord. If only one breaks, the sash will tilt to one side and either jam solid or require a lot of fiddling to get it moving. If both break, the sash can crash down like a guillotine blade in a highly dangerous fashion. Therefore, when making a repair, it is advisable to renew all four sash cords, since if one breaks, the others are likely to follow suit.

Using a blunt chisel, prise off the staff beads. Normally, these are just pinned in place, but paint can make them stubborn, so take care not to break them. Swing the inner sash clear of the frame, prise off the pocket covers – only rarely will these be screwed in place – and pull out the sash weights still attached to the cords (top left) with a stiff wire hook. Cut the cords to free the sash completely, prise off the parting beads and repeat the process for the outer sash. After removing the sashes, use the wire hook to retrieve the weights belonging to the broken cords.

To complete the first stage of the job, vacuum any dust from inside the hollow frame, oil the pulleys, and remove what's left of the cords from the sashes. You should find that each is tacked into a groove running down the side of the sash stile.

When fitting the new cords, tackle the outer sash first. Tie a bent nail to a length of thin string, feed this in over the pulley, and hook it out through the pocket (top right). By tying the string to the sash cord, you can easily pull the cord along the same route. Once the cord has emerged from the pocket, remove the string, and tie on the sash weight originally used in that position. This is important because the weights may have been individually tailored.

Pull the weight up into the frame until it is just below the pulley, and temporarily pin the cord to the side of the frame to hold it. After fitting the sash cord on the other side in exactly the same way, you can cut the cords to length. Holding the sash in position at the top of the window, mark the level of the pulleys on the stiles (bottom left). Lower the sash as far as it will go, then tack the free end of each cord into the groove on the stile, using four or five tacks per side to secure roughly 300 mm (12 in) of cord (bottom right). Make sure that the uppermost tack comes just below the mark indicating the pulley position. Cut the cord just below the last tack, remove the temporary pins from the frame and check that the window slides freely. Finally, replace the pocket covers and parting beads, fit new cords to the inner sash, and replace the staff bead.

## SAFETY

It comes as a shock to many people to discover that, statistically, if they are going to have an accident, the chances are it will happen in their own home. The problem of improving safety in the home can be solved by applying common sense.

Make sure your home is in good repair, particularly floorings, furniture and anything that could fall on someone should its fixings fail. This applies, particularly, to roof tiles, chimney pots, wall cupboards and picture frames.

You should also do your best to ensure that people can see accidents coming. Adequate lighting is important, especially on stairs, but arranging furniture sensibly so that people aren't forced to sit or stand near a door, also helps.

Fire is a major hazard. Check electric leads regularly for faults, and take care when cooking or using open fires; choosing fire-resistant furniture, fabrics and decorations is equally worthwhile. However, in case the worst comes to the worst, install some fire-fighting equipment. Keep a small fire extinguisher – the sort that is safe for electrical fires – and an asbestos blanket in the kitchen, and put smoke detectors in the stairwell, preferably close to the bedrooms.

## STAIRS

Most staircases consist of horizontal treads and vertical risers joined together by triangular timber blocks, and rebated into long side pieces (strings), where they are secured with glue and hardwood wedges. The most common fault is squeaking.

The most likely cause of squeaking is a loose tread, and this is best re-fixed from under the stairs. Begin by checking that the triangular blocks holding the tread to its riser are firmly in place. If they are not, carefully prise them off with a chisel, clean up the timber's surface, and reglue them. If that doesn't work, or if any blocks are missing, reinforce the joint between tread and riser by screwing in metal shelf brackets.

Make sure that both treads and risers fit snugly into the strings. Replace any damaged or missing wedges – you will have to make replacements yourself, using an old wedge as a pattern – and tap them all sharply with a hammer or mallet to check that they are fully home (see bottom left).

Unfortunately, none of this is possible where the underside of the stairs is boarded over, unless, of course, you are prepared to rip off the covering. Here, you must attempt to cure the problem from above. If the squeak is relatively minor, puffing French chalk into the gap between tread and riser sometimes does the trick. Failing that, prise apart the tread and riser enough to squeeze a little woodworking adhesive in between. Then, reinforce the joint with screws driven into the riser's edge through the tread (see bottom right).

Worn nosings – the rounded edges of the treads – are another likely problem. There is, however, no need to replace the entire tread in order to make a repair.

Draw a line parallel to the tread's front edge, immediately above where you judge the riser to be, and using a wide, sharp chisel, carefully cut back the nosing and tread towards this line until half of the riser's thickness is exposed across the entire width of the tread. If there is a moulding beneath the nosing, remove this first, and, if the ends of the riser are rebated into the side strings of the staircase, make a saw cut at each end to free the wood you wish to remove. You may also find that the riser is

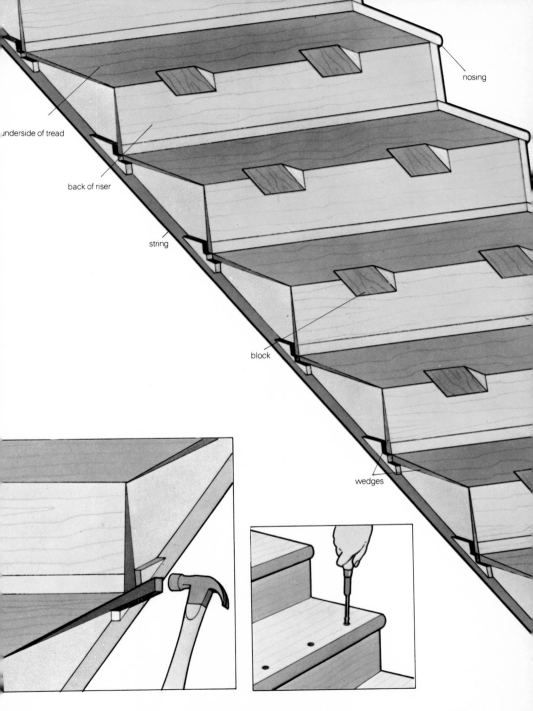

nosing

underside of tread

back of riser

string

block

wedges

43

jointed into the tread; generally with a sort of tongue-and-groove joint. In this case, if necessary, simply chisel off the riser's tongue to leave a neat, straightforward rebate into which a new section of nosing can be fitted.

You will have to make the new nosing yourself from a length of softwood the same thickness as the stair's tread, shaping it to match the old nosing with a plane or Surform. Fix it into the newly cut rebate with glue and screws driven through into the old part of the tread. Drill the necessary clearance and countersink holes for these before fitting the repair patch, and cover the screw heads with filler.

The only other problem you are likely to meet with stairs, is where the string comes loose from the wall. The solution, here, is to drill through the string into the wall and make a new fixing using a long screw and wall plug. The sort of plug/brass screw combination sold for fixing window frames is best.

## VENTILATION

Many people see ventilation as nothing more than a heat waster, something they can well do without, if doing without will reduce their fuel bills. However, when it comes to making your home comfortable, good ventilation is just as important as good heating. It combats condensation, and it ensures the safety and efficiency of fuel-burning appliances. You should aim for a compromise with ventilation, letting sufficient fresh air in, yet preventing the loss of too much warm air.

In reaching that compromise, you need to know how much of the ventilation requirement is met by opening windows, ventilation grilles, air bricks, and draughts. Accurate calculation of this is a job for a professional, but you can reach an acceptable result by trial and error.

Broadly speaking, if after draught-proofing your home (see page 16) a room feels stuffy, or if it suffers from condensation, even temporarily, increase the ventilation by opening a window or two. If that leaves the room feeling uncomfortably cold, or if it is undesirable because you have just spent a lot of money on double glazing, consider installing trickle vents. These air grilles can be slid open or closed, and may be fitted in walls, doors, or window frames. You still need to rely on windows for the bulk of the ventilation, but you will need to open fewer of them, and then only occasionally.

If the window and trickle vent combination fails – as it almost certainly will in kitchens, bathrooms, or utility areas – then you must install a powered extractor fan. Ideally, choose one that will meet the room's total ventilation requirement, and your supplier will help here.

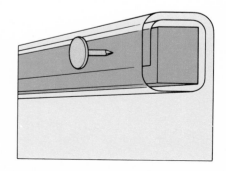

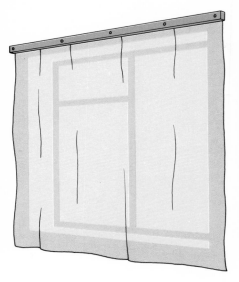

## WINDOWS

Although the problems associated with specific windows (see pages 17, 20 and 38) have been dealt with already, there are a couple of general tips to remember.

Often, the window frame doesn't quite fit the opening in the wall, leaving gaps through which rain and cold air can penetrate. What's more, these gaps are difficult to fill, whether from inside with cellulose filler, or from outside with mortar. This is because window frames tend to shrink or swell according to the weather – timber frames because their moisture content varies; metal and plastic frames because of temperature changes. Mastic filler is sufficiently flexible to accommodate this movement.

Several types of mastic are available; those suitable for exterior use are generally based on silicon rubber.

Before sealing the gap, rake out any old mortar, and clean up the surfaces as much as possible with a wire brush, removing the dust with an old paintbrush. Then, squeeze the mastic from its cartridge with a special applicator gun, aiming to produce a continuous bead around the frame. When you have finished, tidy up the appearance of the mastic by drawing a piece of dowel over it. Dip the dowel in water to stop it sticking.

If you have broken window panes that cannot be fixed immediately, don't just leave them. Keep out the weather, until you can make a proper repair, by covering the window with a sheet of polythene (above).

Secure this around the edges with timber battens temporarily nailed to the window frame (left). For a sound fixing, roll the polythene around the battens before securing them in this way.

45

# DECORATING

## CEILINGS

To paper a ceiling is relatively easy if you approach it in the right way; it is a nightmare if you don't. The main aid to success is the way in which you reach the ceiling. Work from a scaffold board spanning two step ladders, so that you can simply walk from one end of the paper run to the other.

Having sorted out the access, you'll find that papering a ceiling isn't so very different from papering a wall (see page 69). In fact, in some respects, it is easier because there are fewer obstacles to get in the way – normally just a ceiling rose – and only rarely do you have to turn corners. Deciding where to start is easier, too. Traditionally, ceiling

*Above and right:*
*Papering a ceiling.*
*Opposite page:*
*Laying cork tiles*
*(see instructions*
*overleaf).*

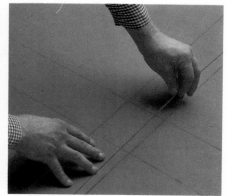

papers are hung working away from, and parallel to, the room's main window in order to stop overlapping joins casting shadows. However, with modern butt-jointed papers, you can start against any wall you think makes papering easier.

Of course, ceilings do present some difficulties. You'll be working against gravity, and you will be handling rather longer pieces of paper than you are used to. Neither should cause much trouble if you take care. Just apply plenty of paste

(see page 57) and fold the paper into an easy-to-handle concertina.

To begin work, remove close-fitting lights (turn off the power first), lampshades, and anything else likely to get in the way. Mark a line parallel to one wall and about 50-75 mm (2-3 in) less than the paper width away from it. This provides a trimming allowance to absorb irregularities where the wall and ceiling meet, and the easiest way to mark it is with a length of string coated in chalk. Stretch this tightly across the ceiling,

47

and snap it against the surface like a bowstring.

Pick up the concertina of pasted paper; you'll find it easy to carry if you drape it over a spare roll of paper. Pull out a couple of folds, and position them so that the end of the paper overlaps the wall by about 75 mm (3 in), and so that its edge runs along the chalk line (top left, page 46). Brush it firmly into place (top right). Then walk back along the scaffold board, gradually pulling out and brushing into place the remaining folds from the concertina of paper until the entire length is up (bottom). If the paper pulls away from the ceiling while you are doing this, try holding the concertina closer to it, and pull out fewer folds at a time. Finally, crease and trim round the edges of the paper in the same way as when papering a wall.

Subsequent lengths are hung in exactly the same way, each butting against its neighbour, until you reach the far side of the room. Here, if the remaining strip of ceiling is substantially narrower than the width of the paper, trim off some of the excess before hanging the length.

Treat ceiling roses in the same way as light switches (see Wallpapering Techniques, page 68). Just remember to drop the pendant flex through the hole.

## CORK TILING

Cork tiles offer one of the simplest ways to cover a floor.

Having made sure that the floor's surface is clean, dry, sound and reasonably level (see page 50), work out how the tiles can best be arranged. Ideally, they should be set out symmetrically, in such a way that any cut tiles needed to fill in around the edges of the floor are at least 50-75 mm (2-3 in) wide. Stretch a chalked string between the mid-points of opposite walls, and snap it down sharply on to the floor to leave two lines which cross at the centre of the floor (top left, page 47). Use these as a guide to dry-lay (without adhesive) two rows of whole tiles in an L-shape from the centre of the room out towards the walls. If the gap left between either of the legs of the 'L' and the wall is too narrow for a cut tile, restrike the guide lines in a slightly different position, and try again (top right, page 47). Once you have found a suitable starting point, begin tiling in earnest.

Apply the adhesive to the floor with a notched spreader, covering roughly 1 m$^2$ at a time, and smooth the tiles into place with a soft cloth, making sure each butts up against its neighbour. Start by laying the four tiles that fit at the junction of the guide lines, and work out towards the walls until you have laid as many whole tiles as possible (bottom left, page 47). Once these are in place, begin filling in the gaps around the edges of the room.

Cutting tiles is very easy. Working on a piece of scrap board, slice through them with a sharp craft knife, using a metal straight-edge as a guide. The hard part is knowing where to cut – you must allow for the fact that the room may not be absolutely square. To overcome this problem, measure the width of the gap at each end, transferring the measurements to the tile and joining them with a straight line. For a quicker method, lay the tile you wish to cut exactly on top of the whole tile that is to be its neighbour, making sure the edges align. Put another whole tile on top, butting one edge against the wall, and use the opposite edge as a guide to draw the cutting line on the tile below (bottom right, page 47).

The latter method is easily adapted to cope with corners (just repeat the process for each wall), but when cutting irregular shapes, it is best to follow a paper pattern. To make such a pattern, take a tile-sized piece of paper and lay it in position on the floor, making freeing cuts in the edges as required until it lays flat. Draw around the obstacle, and cut out the shape.

To complete the job, unless the cork tiles are factory-sealed, protect them with two or three coats of polyurethane varnish. First, vacuum the floor clean, then, with a soft, lint-free cloth, rub in a priming coat diluted with white spirit to the manufacturer's instructions. Allow this to dry before applying two, or more undiluted finishing coats with a brush, letting each dry before applying the next. Throughout this process, your main enemy is dust. If you find the surface marred by dust specks, rub it over lightly with fine wire wool, wipe over with a damp cloth, allow to dry, and try again.

## CROSS-LINING

For a really smooth, professional result, walls should be cross-lined before applying any decorative paint or paper finish. This involves covering the wall with horizontal lengths of cheap lining paper to absorb the lumps and bumps.

The main reason for hanging the paper horizontally is that when you cover it with a vertically hung wall-covering, the two sets of joins don't coincide, making for a flatter, more durable finish. If the lining is to be painted, this does not matter so much, but even here the horizontal approach is generally best. Generally, it means fewer joins between lengths of paper, which in turn makes the lining much less obvious.

It isn't difficult to cross-line a wall. After all, any minor mistakes will be covered up by the paint or finished wallcovering. Tackle it in the same way as preparing a ceiling (see page 46). Cut the paper into lengths, allowing roughly 75 mm (3 in) extra at each end for trimming, paste them generously, and fold them into conveniently-sized concertinas.

Measure down from the ceiling to a distance equal to 50 mm (2 in) less than the width of the paper and mark the wall. Stretch a length of chalked string along the wall, at the same height as the mark, and 'snap' it to leave a guide line for the edge of the first paper length. If you want to be really fussy – and it is worth it if the lining is to be painted – check that this guide line is absolutely horizontal with a spirit level.

Now, hold the paper concertina in your left hand, pull out a couple of folds and, having lined up the edge with the guide line, brush the paper firmly into place. Continue by working backwards along the wall, opening out the concertina a few folds at a

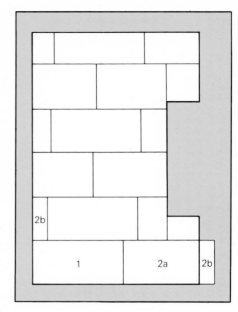

time, and brushing the paper into place as you go (above). As with papering ceilings, this is easier if you work from a scaffold board between two step ladders.

Once the length of paper is in place, trim it to fit. At the ends of the wall allow a 50 mm (2 in) overlap to paste on to the adjacent wall. When you paper this second wall, trim the lining to fit right into the corner, covering the overlap. This gives a neat finish even if the walls are out of true. Hang subsequent lengths in the same manner, butting each against its neighbour.

## FLOOR LEVELLING

Solid floors are easiest to level, and the best method is to use a self-levelling flooring compound or screed. Looking a bit like runny plaster, this is poured on to the surface and roughly levelled to a maximum thickness of 3 mm (⅛ in) with a steel float. Like all liquids, it then settles to a perfectly flat, level finish. If a thicker layer is needed, apply extra coats, allowing each to harden for about

12 hours before applying the next. Finally, leave it for two or three days before laying a new floor covering.

Floorboards need a different approach. Cover them with 1220 × 600 mm (4 × 2 ft) sheets of hardboard. Before laying the board, brush water into the rough side of each sheet, and leave them stacked back to back in the room in which they will be laid for two or three days. This ensures that the hardboard will not absorb moisture, swell and buckle.

Go over the floor, punching down nail heads, and refixing loose boards (see Floorboards page 19). Lay a row of sheets along one wall, fixing each in place with 25 mm (1 in) annular or screw nails. These have ribbed or twisted shanks respectively, which stop them coming loose. Set the nails roughly 230 mm (9 in) apart; 150 mm

(6 in) apart round the edges.

Cut the last board in the row to fit, and use the off-cut to start the next row (left). This reduces wastage, and helps the levelling by staggering the joins brick-fashion. Continue in this way until the floor is completely covered. Then, vacuum it clean. If an obstacle interrupts a row, don't bother fitting a sheet around it. Cut the board off squarely to cover as much of the floor as possible, and fill in with off-cuts when the rest of the floor has been dealt with.

## CERAMIC FLOOR TILING

*Ensure a right-angle with two wooden battens.*

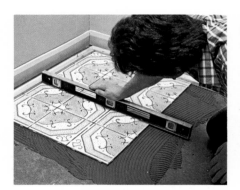

*Constantly check that the tiles are level during the work.*

*Remove the wooden battens and fill in with cut tiles.*

*Apply the adhesive to the backs of these tiles.*

*Apply the grout over all the tiles and polish the tile surface when dry.*

51

## FLOOR TILING

If you are looking for a flooring that is hardwearing, easy to keep clean, and unaffected by water, you won't do any better than ceramic floor tiles. They are ideal for kitchens, utility areas, and, of course, bathrooms.

When laying ceramic tiles (see page 51), you should prepare the floor thoroughly, making sure it is clean, dry, sound and level. If tiling over floorboards, level them with 10 mm (⅜ in) thick plywood, not hardboard. You must also prepare inward-opening room doors. Remove them and plane their bottom edges to accommodate the new floor level after tiling.

Setting out is done in the same way as for cork tiles (see page 48), but accuracy is far more important. Remember to leave gaps between tiles for the grouting, using matchstick spacers. Having found the best arrangement, temporarily nail a timber batten to the floor and parallel to one wall, its inner edge corresponding to the inner edges of the border tiles. Position a second batten in the same way parallel to the adjacent wall, ensuring that together they form a perfect right-angle. To check this, measure outwards from the corner joint and make a mark on one batten 3 m (3 ft 3 in) from the join. Mark a point on the other batten 4 m (13 ft) from the join and measure the diagonal between the two points; if the battens are at right-angles, this will be exactly 5 m (16 ft 3 in). In fact, you can choose any unit of measurement you like for this check; if one is 3, and the other 4, then the third should be 5.

Apply a thin bed of flooring adhesive with a notched spreader, covering an area big enough for nine tiles. Starting at the angle between the battens, press the tiles into place, spacing them apart with matchsticks and using a spirit level to check they are both level and flush with their neighbours. Continue in this way until all that remains is to remove the edge battens and fill in with cut tiles. You will find it easier to apply the adhesive to the backs of these.

Mark them up, using one of the methods described for cork tiles (see page 48), and draw a tile cutter along the mark. Follow a straight edge, and score right through the glaze, including any on the tile edges. If you lay the tile face up with a couple of matchsticks immediately beneath the scored line, firm pressure should snap it cleanly in two. More complex shapes are cut in the same way as wall tiles (see page 73).

Leave the floor undisturbed for a day, before removing the matchstick spacers, and applying grout.

## GROUTING

Grouting means filling the gaps between ceramic tiles with a special compound, called grout. Some grouts are flexible, some splashproof, some extra waterproof to stand total immersion, and some are easy-to-clean epoxy types for use on worktops. However, most are plain white and cement-based.

Grout comes as a powder that you mix with water to a thick cream and press between the tiles with a plastic spreader. Don't worry if, in the process, you get it on the face of the tiles.

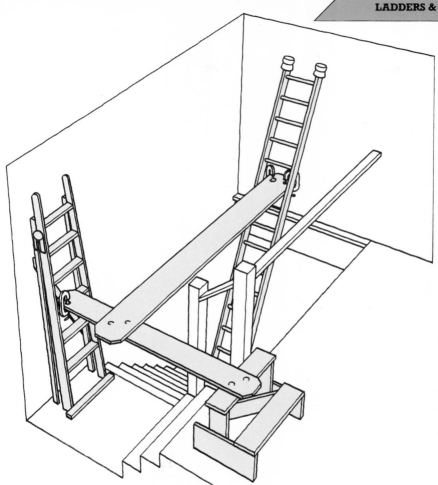

The main thing is to fill those gaps. Having treated a reasonable area, run over the joins with your finger to tidy them up; wear rubber gloves to stop the cement irritating your skin. Then, continue until the whole of the tiled area has been grouted. Leave the grout overnight, and then wash off the excess with plenty of clean water. Repeat the process until only a fine white 'bloom' remains, and polish this off with a soft clean cloth.

## LADDERS & STEPS

The basic rules for using ladders and steps indoors are the same as for using them outside (see page 30). Safety must be your first priority, so ensure that they will remain stable by setting them on a firm, level base, and taking precautions to stop them slipping. However, where decorating is concerned, safety alone is not enough. You must be able to work in

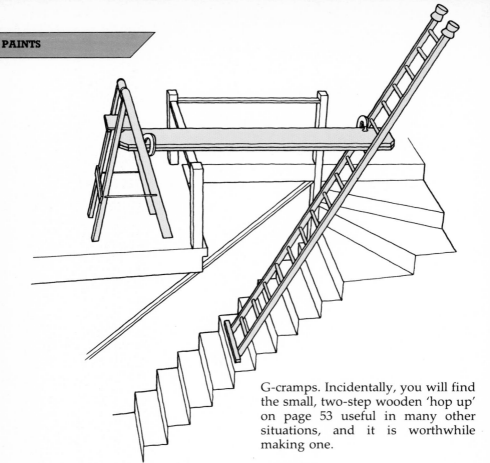

G-cramps. Incidentally, you will find
the small, two-step wooden 'hop up'
on page 53 useful in many other
situations, and it is worthwhile
making one.

## PAINTS

Broadly speaking, paints fall into
three categories: the resin-based suc-
cessors to old-fashioned oil paints,
emulsions, and what could be
termed 'special finishes'.

Resin-based paints are primarily
for wood and metal, though they
can be used on walls with the correct
preparation. Most give a gloss finish,
but semi-gloss (eggshell) and matt
versions are also to be found.

Emulsions are mainly for walls and
ceilings. Generally, they give a matt
or semi-gloss finish (the latter known
as silk or satin – the name varies), but

comfort, and, for many jobs, you will
need to retain a degree of mobility.

In most cases, this can be achieved
by laying a scaffold board between a
couple of step ladders – the extra ladder and the board can be hired.
However, stairwells present special
problems. The safest way to overcome them is with an arrangement
like that shown on page 53, or that
shown above – choose whichever fits
your stair layout. Notice how battens
screwed temporarily to the floor stop
ladders and steps slipping, and how
the scaffold boards are secured with

a few gloss emulsions are available.

The greatest variety is in special paints. Some are alternatives to gloss or emulsion, offering a special feature. There are, for example, non-drip (thixotropic) versions of both, glosses that are water-soluble just like emulsion, and glosses such as the polyurethanes that give an extra-hard finish. The names of the rest are more or less self explanatory. Emulsions for exterior use call themselves exterior emulsions; floor paint is called floor paint; and so on.

*Paint brush techniques.*

## PAINTING TECHNIQUES

There are three main techniques for

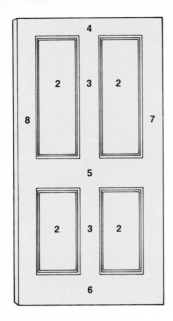

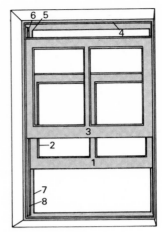

Sash window

applying paint, and the one you choose depends mainly on the sort of finish you wish to achieve.

For a smooth gloss finish, stir the paint thoroughly, and strain it through an old pair of tights, or something similar, into a separate container, ideally a proper paint kettle. Non-drip paints should now be left to regain their jelly-like consistency. When you are ready to paint, dust the surface with an old dry brush, and remove dust from your paint brush by flicking the bristles through your fingers. Dip the brush into the paint, immersing roughly half the length of the bristles, and squeeze out the excess paint against the inside of the container (page 55).

If painting wood, apply the paint in the direction of the grain, spacing the strokes a little way apart. As the brush begins to run dry, blend the strokes together by working across them, as shown on page 55. Finally, lightly run the brush over the surface in the direction of the grain. Reload it with paint and move on to the next patch.

With most paints, the first coat will not give very good results. In particular, any original colour may well show through. Don't try to overcome this by applying thicker coats. It's better to leave the first coat to dry, rub it down lightly with fine glasspaper, and apply another coat on top, repeating the process until the desired finish is achieved.

When painting edges, always work the brush out towards them. If you work in from the edge, you will get a build up of paint around the angle. If your hand isn't very steady, and you want to paint up to a line, protect the surface you don't want painted with masking tape or with a paint shield – a thin piece of metal or

actually taking the window apart.

Non-gloss finishes require a less stringent technique. Prepare the paint and load the brush as described previously, applying it to the surface by working it back and forth across a central point in a rough star pattern (left). This ensures that dips and bumps in the surface don't produce unpainted 'shadows'. When the brush begins to run dry, simply re-load, and paint another star next to, and overlapping, the first. Continue in this way until all that remains is to fill in at the edges. Tackle these more carefully. You may actually find it easier to paint around the edges first, using a smaller brush to create a sort of safety zone – a painted border about 150 mm (6 in) wide. Then, you can work outwards to this without having to worry about paint splashing on to adjacent surfaces.

You can also use the 'star' method when painting with a roller, but you will definitely need to paint a 'safety zone' with a brush first. Take care not to work the roller back and forth too quickly, otherwise paint may spray off in all directions. The technique for loading a roller is obviously rather different than for a brush. Strain the paint into a roller tray, making sure the tray's ramp is left reasonably clear, run the roller into the paint and remove the excess by running it over the ramp.

## PASTE & PASTING

Paste is used to hold wallcoverings in place, and there are several types available. They are sold either ready-mixed in a tub, or in powder form for mixing with water, and the one you

card, held in your free hand. When painting window frames, though, you should allow the final coat of paint to overlap the glass by about 3 mm (⅛ in). This prevents water getting under the paint film.

When painting complicated surfaces, such as panelled doors and window frames, tackle the various sections in a logical order. The order for painting a panelled door is given opposite, and it can be adapted to cope with casement windows – just imagine the door panels are glass.

Sash windows are more of a problem. Start by pushing up the bottom sash and pulling down the top one. This way you can paint the bottom section of the top sash, the whole of the bottom sash, and the otherwise inaccessible parts of the window frame. Leave these to dry, return the sashes to their normal positions, and finish off the top sash. When this is dry, simply manoeuvre the sashes to gain access to as much of the remaining frame as you can reach without

choose depends on the wallcovering. For ordinary wallpapers, almost any paste will do, and although you may get away with ordinary paste mixed to a thicker-than-normal consistency for heavyweight papers, a heavy-duty paste is better. Vinyl wallcoverings, and other impervious finishes, need a paste containing a fungicide to prevent mould developing behind them. Also, there are a number of special pastes designed for use with special wallcoverings such as hessian, Novamura, and so on.

You will find pasting a lot easier if you have the right equipment: a purpose-made pasting table, a paste brush, a bucket with string tied between the handle retaining lugs (to scrape off excess paste and support the brush when not in use), and a stick for stirring.

Mix the paste in the bucket following the manufacturer's instructions. Then, cut the wallcovering into suitable lengths – remembering to allow 50-75 mm (2-3 in) extra at each end for trimming – and arrange the first length to be pasted on the pasting table with one end and its far edge overhanging by about 25 mm (1 in). Charge the brush, scrape off the excess, and apply the paste, working out from the centre towards the end and far edge of the paper. Never drag the brush back over the edge or you will get paste on the patterned side. Aim for an even, generous coat, making sure you don't miss any patches and removing any lumps that may appear as you go.

Next, move the paper so that the near edge overhangs, paste out to that, and fold the pasted section in half to bring the pasted surfaces together. Move the paper along, and treat the rest of it in the same way. How you fold the remaining paper depends on its length. Long pieces should be folded concertina fashion in easy-to-handle small sections. With pieces up to the height of the average wall, you need only one additional fold, making two in all: a short initial fold at the top, and a long second fold for the rest.

## PLASTER PREPARATION
When preparing a plaster wall for decoration, the main task is to fill in all cracks and holes, using cellulose filler, or a semi-flexible mastic called caulking around window and door frames (see Windows page 45).

Rake out cracks with the corner of a filling knife (top left), undercutting the surrounding material to provide a 'key' for the filler. Brush out any loose dust, and then brush water into the crack (top right). Press in the filler (bottom left), scraping off most, but not all, of the excess. Leave the filler slightly proud of the wall to allow for shrinkage as it dries. When dry, sand it smooth with medium- or fine-grade glasspaper (bottom right).

Holes can be tackled in the same way, but if they are on the large side, the filler may tend to sag. The answer is to fill the hole in stages, allowing each layer to dry. This doesn't overcome the problem of cost, however; filler is really too expensive for large repairs. One way out is to fill the bulk of the hole with a cheap plaster such as Sirapite. For quicker results, soak newspaper in plaster, ram it into the hole, and top with filler.

## PREPARATION

Good though modern decorating materials are, they cannot work miracles. That's why thorough preparation is so necessary to remove all those lumps, bumps and cracks which will spoil the new decor. In general terms, what you must aim for is a surface that is dry, sound, reasonably smooth, and clean, in that order.

Obviously, the surface shouldn't show any sign of moisture, whether condensation, dew, rain or washing water. More importantly, the structure must be free from inherent dampness (see page 11).

A sound surface is harder to define. Clearly, rotten woodwork, rusty metalwork, and walls or ceilings which are cracked, full of holes, or on the verge of collapse, should be repaired. However, there are less obvious examples of unsound surfaces. If the surface is slightly dusty – in other words, it leaves a deposit on your skin when you run your hand over it – few decorations will stick. In this case, it must be bound together, using a stabilizing primer. If the surface already has some form of decoration, whether you strip this off or leave it depends on what it is and on what you use to cover it.

Paint can be left if it is in good condition. Scrape off any that is loose or flaking, fill the resulting hollows with cellulose filler, and rub down with glasspaper. On the other hand, if it has been applied badly, is too thick for doors and windows to open properly, or is in generally poor shape, strip it off and start again. The only complication is rust. To deal with this, strip off loose paint, and rub back to bright metal with wire wool or coarse 'wet-and-dry' paper. Treat the affected area with a proprietary anti-rust agent, then fill in the pitting with a car body filler before priming and painting.

Vinyl and old-fashioned washable wallcoverings should be removed. However, ordinary wallpapers, textured wallcovering, and the backing paper left after the first stage of stripping certain vinyls, can be left if they are clean and well stuck down. There are risks, though, as the inks used on some papers may 'bleed' through new decorations. More importantly, there is a chance that the water in new wallpaper paste, or in emulsion paint, may soften the old paste, encouraging the paper to lift, blister, or actually peel.

Any surfaces that aren't smooth after making the necessary running repairs should be sanded down.

Always wash down the surface just before decorating. Use plenty of warm water and detergent, and take off most of the dirt by working your way up from the bottom of the wall. Change the water, then rinse off the detergent, working down from the top. Finally, dry the surface with a soft, lint-free cloth, or simply leave it to dry – the latter may leave smears if you live in a hard-water area.

## PRIMERS & UNDERCOATS

Few paints will stick to a 'virgin' surface unless it has been sealed with a primer. There are many types depending on the material being treated, so choose the one you need from the table opposite. When you use a primer, remember it is only a sealant, so a thin coat is all that is necessary.

Undercoats are another matter. These simple, resin-based matt paints are designed to obliterate whatever is beneath them, thus saving on the amount of resin-based top coat needed for a good finish. Apply them in the same way as you would ordinary gloss.

## STRIPPING PAINT

Basically, there are two ways to strip paint: one is to use a blowlamp; the other is to use a chemical paint stripper. Many people worry about using blowlamps, but modern gas models are very safe. They strip paint quickly, and they are relatively cheap to run.

You'll need thick gloves, a flat scraper for plain surfaces, and a shavehook (preferably a combination model) for mouldings and awkward corners. Play the blowlamp's flame

## CHOOSING THE RIGHT PRIMER

| Surface | Primer |
| --- | --- |
| Bare softwood and man-made board | Wood primer, all-surface primer, or primer undercoat. |
| Hardwoods and resinous softwood | Aluminium wood primer. |
| Insulation board | Stabilizing primer. |
| Plastic-faced boards | All-surface primer. |
| Plaster, plasterboard and masonry | All-surface primer under resin-based paints; none under emulsion. |
| Porous or powdery masonry, etc. | Stabilizing primer. |
| Old wallcovering | Treat any metallic sections of the design with knotting. |
| Lining papers and relief wallcoverings | None under emulsion; a thinned coat of emulsion under resin-based paint. |
| Aluminium | Zinc chromate or zinc phosphate primer; NOT lead-based primers. |
| Ferrous metals | Calcium plumbate out of doors; zinc chromate indoors. |
| Galvanized iron and steel | Calcium Plumbate primer. |
| Bitumen-coated metal | Aluminium spirit-based primer. |
| Lead | None needed, but allow to weather. |
| Copper and brass | No primer necessary. |
| Asbestos | All-surface primer, or stabilizing primer if porous. |
| Ceramic tiles | All-surface primer or zinc chromate. |
| Plastic, glassfibre, etc. | All-surface primer. |
| Other surfaces | All-surface primer works on most. |

lightly over the paint until you see this soften and blister, but remove it before it begins to char or set light to the surface below. Then, scrape off the softened paint with whichever tool is appropriate (overleaf, top left). Don't worry if you don't remove all the paint in one go. Reapply the flame and try again. Small specks, and paint trapped in mouldings, however, are best removed with glasspaper or wire wool. You will char the surrounding bare wood if you use the blowlamp on these.

For safety, you must obey a few simple rules when using a blowlamp. Sweep up stripped paint before it becomes a fire hazard, and don't let it drop on to your skin – it will be hot. Protect the floor with dust sheets, not polythene, and be careful where you point the flame when not pointing at

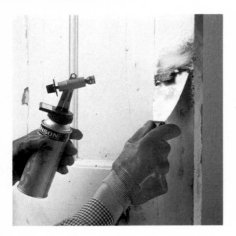

nish; some charring of the wood is inevitable. In these situations, use a chemical stripper.

The cheapest kind is a gel that can be neutralized with water. Using an old paint brush, apply it thhickly with a stabbing action and leave it for as long as possible before scraping off the resulting mush (bottom left). If the paint is very thick, further applications may be necessary. Paint trapped in mouldings is the most difficult to remove; scrub it out with wire wool dipped in paint stripper. When you have finished, rinse the surface with plenty of clean water and sand smooth.

Do remember that paint stripper is strong stuff. Therefore, safety is just as important as when using a blowlamp. Always wear thick rubber gloves, and if stripper or stripped paint should come into contact with your skin, wash it off quickly with plenty of water. Protect floors and furniture, too, using dust sheets; not plastic. Finally, provide plenty of ventilation, and don't let the fumes come into contact with anything hot, including cigarettes. This is not because they are explosive, but because they turn into a poisonous gas. (For this reason, make sure you do not use a blowlamp and paint stripper at the same time.)

## STRIPPING WALLPAPER

When removing old wallpaper, you need a bucket, a large wall brush, the scraper set used for paint stripping, and lots of water.

Thoroughly wet ordinary paper, allowing the water time to soak in and soften the paste. Then, try

the paint. Turn the blowlamp off if you want to stop for a few minutes, and keep pets and children well away.

There are, however, some jobs where blowlamps are not suitable. Never use them on metal because the heat may distort it or alter its temper. Never use them near glass, or the glass may crack, and avoid using them on surfaces you intend to var-

scraping off a trial patch. If it proves stubborn, resoak the paper, and wait a little longer. Do be careful not to dig into the plaster and damage it when scraping, and don't labour too long at trying to remove tiny flecks. Often, these come off more easily if you scrub the wall hard with a scrubbing brush. Failing that, remove them with glasspaper.

Impervious wallcoverings, such as vinyls and old-fashioned washables, present more of a problem, because they don't let the water through to the paste. Some vinyls overcome this by allowing you to peel off the top layer of vinyl and leave a layer of ordinary paper beneath, so it's worth seeing if a corner of the vinyl will lift. If it won't, all you can do is break through the impervious surface by force. A serrated scraper (called a Scarsden scraper) is best here. Drag it over the surface to leave enough scratches for the water to penetrate. Alternatively, make a scraper by driving panel pins through some scrap plywood. Be careful not to apply so much pressure that you cut right through to the wall.

## TEXTURED FINISHES

There is one major exception to the rule that decoration doesn't hide faults – the textured finish. As long as the surface is structurally sound, clean, and free from damp, this will produce an attractive finish, no matter how many minor imperfections the surface may have.

Basically, this is a plaster-style product, normally white, with the consistency of cake icing. Applied to the surface with a brush, float, or spatula, the material is worked to a decorative texture by various means. These include stippling with a sponge wrapped in plastic, stroking with a coarse brush or comb, or running over the top with a roller bound in coarse string.

There are several different types of textured finish, the most obvious difference between them being that some come ready-mixed in tubs, while others are sold as a powder to which you add water. The latter is the cheapest. In most cases, the finish must be painted to colour it, and to protect it from airborne moisture. However, you will find self-coloured versions, washables, and even a few suitable for exterior use.

## TEXTURED WALLCOVERINGS

Another way to give a wall or ceiling a textured finish is to use a textured wallcovering.

The cheapest are the embossed wallpapers, and these have the advantage of being easily removed if you tire of the design – they come off like any other wallpaper. Painting them, however, is a risky business, and they tend not to cover anything more than minor defects, so perhaps a heavier, more deeply embossed wallcovering is a better bet.

The most popular is Anaglypta: essentially a very stiff embossed wallpaper, in pleasant designs or plain, bulked out with cotton. It is designed to be painted – it really needs the protection, and is more or less permanent. There is also a heavy-duty version called Supaglypta, but this is usually only available through trade outlets.

## TILES

Ceramic tiles offer one of the most durable, easy-care finishes for walls, floors, and worktops, but it is important that you choose the right type of tile for the job.

You must use wall tiles on walls, and floor tiles on floors or worktops. The latter are thicker – about 8 mm ($\frac{5}{16}$ in) as opposed to 4 mm ($\frac{5}{32}$ in) – and better able to withstand stress. For outdoor use, you must also ensure that the tiles are frost-resistant.

When choosing, consider the way in which the tile is made. The majority of modern tiles are 'universal'. In other words, you may use the same tile for edging as for the rest of the job. A few ranges, however, offer 'field' tiles (tiles with square, unglazed edges) designed to cover the bulk of the area, plus 'edging' tiles with glazed edges to finish off the perimeter. Unfortunately, some imported tiles are sold only in field tile form. Here, you must find some other means of tidying the edges, quadrant tiles (similar to quadrant wooden mouldings) being a possibility.

Shape and size should also be considered. The majority of wall tiles are either 108 or 152 mm (4¼ or 6 in) square; floor tiles are either 100 or 200 mm (roughly 4 or 8 in) square. Other sizes are to be found, though. For something different, look for oblong tiles, tiles with ornate interlocking shapes, and mini mosaics.

It is worth remembering that, in addition to plain tiles and tiles with self-contained patterns, there is an increasing selection of motifs built up from four-, six-, or nine-tile sets.

## TOOLS

Unfortunately, there is no such thing as a universal decorating tool kit that will cope with every job. Consequently, you will have to collect a number of 'specialized' kits to handle individual tasks as you come to them.

The first task to consider is preparation. You need a plastic bucket, rubber gloves, sponges, a scrubbing brush, and lint-free cloth for washing surfaces. For rubbing down paint and other surfaces, use sheets of silicon carbide abrasive (dry like glasspaper, or wet to increase its life and reduce clogging) or glasspaper (this tends to do a better job on bare wood and plaster). Buy both in a mixture of grades: a few very coarse and fine sheets, plus quite a number of medium grade.

To fill cracks or holes in walls and woodwork, you need two filling knives: one 25 mm (1 in) wide for small jobs; the other 75 mm (3 in) wide. A spearpoint putty knife is also useful for filling in awkward corners, as well as for repairing old putty, and it is worth investing in a small trowel for filling very large holes, or repairing pointing. A mastic applicator gun is another worthwhile, though little used, tool. Of course, you'll need something on which to mix plaster, filler, and mortar. Scrap hardboard will do for the mixing, but for carrying the filler to the job, buy or make a plasterer's hawk – essentially a square board with a central handle underneath.

Finally, you need some tools for stripping paint and paper; a flat scraper (it looks like a filling knife but has a stiffer blade), a shavehook (preferably a combination model), and a blowlamp are the minimum you can get away with. If using a chemical paint stripper, add thick rubber gloves, an old paint brush, and an ordinary saucer into which you can pour the stripper. Get a serrated Scarsden scraper for stripping vinyl and washable wallcoverings.

Painting tools come next, and a set of brushes is a must. One 25 mm (1 in) wide, and another 50 mm (2 in) wide will cope with most woodwork, though it is worth adding a 12 mm (½ in) wide brush for fiddly bits. For walls and other large areas, choose a 100 or 125 mm (4 or 5 in) brush. Don't buy very cheap brushes; they don't last, and they don't give good results. If you want quick, throwaway paint applicators, try paint pads. These are better than they used to be, but the finish still won't be of very high quality. Equally, don't pay a fortune for professional-quality brushes. You will find these difficult to use, and it will take you years just to 'break them in'.

A roller set is a good investment, particularly if you expect to do a lot of wall and ceiling painting. It should comprise a roller tray, roller frame, and a selection of spare sleeves. Avoid cheap foam plastic sleeves. Go for mohair or synthetic fibre (imitation mohair) sleeves if dealing with reasonably smooth surfaces; sheepskin sleeves if dealing with rough or textured surfaces.

Last, but not least, there are wallpapering tools. Here, the basics are a pasting table, a paste brush, a pair of long-bladed scissors, a tape measure, a plumb-line and bob, a pencil, a seam roller, and a paperhanging brush. A really sharp craft knife will also come in handy. If using ready-pasted wallcoverings, dispense with the pasting table and paperhanging brush; instead, buy a soaking trough and sponge.

## VINYL FLOORING

Sheet vinyl flooring is an excellent choice for kitchens, bathrooms, utility rooms, and hallways. It's durable, easy to keep clean, and softer and warmer than most alternatives, particularly the cushioned types. It comes in a range of designs, including tile effects, and it is relatively inexpensive.

Before laying the vinyl, make sure the floor is dry, sound, clean, and relatively flat. Loosen the roll slightly, and leave it for a few hours in the room in which it is to be used. Switch the heating on. As the vinyl warms up, it will soften and become more pliable. When ready, unroll the vinyl fully and manoeuvre it roughly into place so it lies as flat as possible, a 100-125 mm (4-5 in) overlap turning up each wall. This is to allow for the fact that the room may not be absolutely square.

Make a 45-degree cut across each overlap to allow you to push the vinyl right into the corner of the room (bottom right page 66). Many rooms contain window bays, chimney breasts, and other awkward features to interrupt the unrolling, so you must fit the vinyl roughly around these obstructions by making freeing cuts (bottom left page 66).

When faced with a square window

*With a pencil and wooden block spacer, scribe the trimming line on the vinyl flooring.*

*Following the trimming line, remove the waste using a sharp knife, such as a Stanley knife.*

bay, make freeing cuts in line with each side of the bay to produce a sort of flap that will fall into place.

The bulk of the waste overlapping the main walls can, for convenience, be removed to await final trimming. The snag is that such a simple flap leaves no trimming allowance for the bay's side walls, which may lead to trouble if the bay is out of square. To

overcome this, make the freeing cuts at an angle so the flap is a dovetail shape.

In most cases, exactly the same principles apply with more complex shapes – you just need more freeing cuts. To get round a simple chimney breast, for example, first make freeing cuts to fit the vinyl around the hearth and fire surround. Having

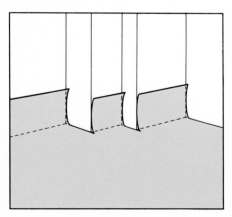

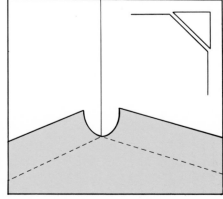

Overlap sheets to be joined and cut through their combined thickness so that you have a fitting edge.

Peel back the vinyl and remove the waste from both pieces in readiness for applying the adhesive.

Spread a band of adhesive on the floor along the line of the join with a suitable scraper.

To complete the join, merely smooth the vinyl firmly back into place with your hand.

trimmed off the bulk of the waste here, make another set of freeing cuts to drop the vinyl into the alcoves at each side.

Leave the vinyl to settle down for as long as possible before final trim-ming. There are two ways to trim vinyl. The simplest is similar to trim-ming wallpaper. You merely push a wooden block along the angle be-tween floor and wall to crease the vinyl, lift it clear, and remove the

67

waste by running a sharp knife along the crease. Unfortunately, this only works well on thin, soft vinyls. On thicker floorings, you must use a technique called scribing. Pull the vinyl away from the wall so that it lies flat and its edge is parallel to the skirting board. Mark it by running a pencil over it, keeping a constant distance from the skirting by using a piece of scrap wood as a spacer (top left page 66). This will reproduce any undulations in the skirting, and so give an accurate cutting line.

If the manufacturer recommends that the vinyl be stuck down, leave it for a few days after trimming to settle. Then, peel back the edges, apply a band of flooring adhesive to the floor, and smooth the vinyl back into place. In heavy traffic areas, stick it down over the entire floor. In this case, smooth it down by dragging something heavy across it – a plastic sack filled with sand, for example.

If you need to join two lengths of vinyl, try to arrange for the join to fall in a position where it won't be too noticeable, and where it won't be subject to heavy wear. Overlap the two sheets to be joined, so that their patterns match exactly. This is best done before trimming the vinyl around the room's walls. Then, using a straight-edge as a guide, cut through both thicknesses at the same time (top left page 67). Removing the waste from each piece (top right page 67) will leave a perfectly matching butt joint that can be stuck down to hold it in place.

The most accurate way to trim round awkward-shaped items is with a pattern. Roughly cut a sheet of paper to fit around the obstacle, and then use the scribing technique described previously to copy the obstacle's shape on to the paper. By laying the paper on the vinyl and reversing the scribing process, you will be left with an outline to cut round. If the hole isn't on the edge of a sheet, make a straight cut out to the nearest edge so that the vinyl can be slipped round the obstacle.

## WALLPAPERING TECHNIQUES
Before deciding where the first length of paper or 'drop' is to be hung, apply a coat of paste or 'size' to the bare walls and allow it to dry. Where possible, choose to start hanging paper at the end of a long, plain wall, to get the feel of the job, before tackling anything difficult.

Use a plumb-line to aid in drawing a vertical line on the wall to indicate the position of the first drop's edge. The distance between this line and the end of the wall should be about 50 mm (2 in) less than the width of the paper. This provides a trimming allowance in case the wall is out of true.

Measure the length of the drop, adding 50-75 mm (2-3 in) top and bottom for trimming, and cut the paper into suitable lengths. With patterned papers, cut the first piece to size, lay it patterned side up on the pasting table, and unroll the next stretch of paper over it. Then, matching the pattern, use the first piece as a guide to cut the second length. Repeat, as necessary, using each preceding length as a cutting guide for the one that follows it.

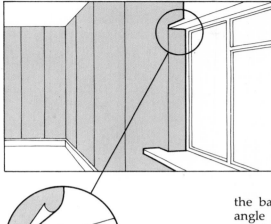

*The narrow gap left on the underside of the reveal is filled with a small offcut.*

Paste several drops (see Paste and Pasting) and leave to become pliable; the paper manufacturer will normally specify a soaking time. Work out a rota so that by the time you have pasted the last drop in the batch, the first will be ready to hang.

You are now ready to start hanging the cut wallpaper. Take the first drop, open out the top fold, and hold it against the wall with its edge against the guide line, and the trimming allowance at the top overlaping on to the ceiling. Brush it on to the wall with the paperhanging brush, working up, out, and down from the centre to avoid trapping air bubbles. Continue down the wall, opening out the lower fold (or folds) and brushing the paper into place in the same way.

To trim the paper accurately, run the back of your scissors along the angle between wall and ceiling, creasing the paper. Pull the paper away from the wall slightly and cut it along the crease. Finally, brush it back into place, applying a little more paste if necessary to make it stick.

Subsequent drops are hung in the same way. The only complication is in matching patterns. Do not try for a perfect match when you first offer the paper up to the wall. Wait until the drop has been brushed out, then slide it into position, applying overall pressure with the palms of both hands. Sizing and generous pasting make this easier.

The technique for applying ready-pasted wallcoverings is only slightly different. Here, instead of pasting each length, soak the paper in the special water trough. With the trough positioned at the foot of the wall, pull out the paper, offer it up to the wall, and smooth it into place with a sponge. To speed up the process – soaking takes time – immerse a number of drops in, say, the bath, and transfer them to the trough as required.

*Paste the paper generously and leave to soak until reasonably supple. It should not be so wet that it tears.*

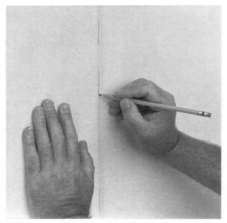

*With a plumb-line made of string, carefully draw a line where the edge of the first drop is to go.*

*Now brush the first drop into place, taking care not to trap any air bubbles by brushing from the centre out.*

paper at the centre of the switch, and make cuts out towards the edges in a star shape. Make a cut towards each corner for a square switch. For round switches, the more cuts, the better. These freeing cuts enable you to brush the rest of the drop on to the wall. Then, it is simply a case of creasing and trimming in the usual way. For a really professional finish, loosen the switch's face plate so you can tuck the edges behind it.

Turning corners is another problem, because walls are often out of true. The trick is to turn no more than about 25 mm (1 in) around internal corners, and about 50 mm (2 in) around external corners. Hang the off-cut, or a new drop, on the second

Minor obstacles, such as light switches, are easy to deal with. Brush out the paper above the switch, and let the rest hang loosely over it. Carefully poke the scissors through the

wall to overlap the paper turning the corner. Check that the edge of this second drop is vertical with a plumb-line. Obviously, you should try to match any pattern, but in practice,

*Crease the paper where it meets the ceiling or skirting and trim to fit with sharp, long-bladed scissors.*

*At corners, measure the distance from the edge of the last drop. Use a plumb-line again in case the corner isn't square.*

*When filling in a space before a corner, cut the drop to the correct width so that it turns the corner by about 25 mm (1 in).*

*Finally, cover the turn with the offcut, or a new drop, ensuring that this is vertical. Make sure the edges are well pasted.*

a perfect match is rarely possible. Fortunately, slight discrepancies won't show and modern wallpapers do make it easier.

That leaves windows and doors.

Where a drop overlaps a corner, remove the bulk of the waste, and make a freeing cut towards the corner of the frame. Brush out the paper and trim it as normal.

71

This will not work if the window is set in a reveal (page 69). Here, make two horizontal cuts through the drop where it overlaps the reveal – one in line with the top of the window sill, and the other 25 mm (1 in) below the soffit. Brush the paper beneath the window into place, and turn the resulting flap on to the side of the reveal. If necessary, hang another drop to finish covering the reveal's side. The next step is to cover the end portion of the soffit with a patch, turning it about 25 mm (1 in) down on to the side of the reveal, and the same amount on to the wall above the window. Tuck these turns under the main drop. The rest of the wall, above and below the window, is now papered normally, turning the paper above the window to cover the soffit. If the window is out of square in relation to the wall, however, cover the soffit separately with patches hung at right-angles to the frame. Turn these on to the wall above by 25 mm, covering the turns with the main drops.

## WALL TILING

If you have taken care over the preparation, wall tiling should not present any undue problems. However, you can make life still easier by working out a tile arrangement that not only looks good, but also avoids the need to use too many awkward shapes. This is called setting out.

The name of the game is symmetry, so begin by drawing a vertical line through the mid-point of the room's most prominent wall, using a plumb-line and a long, straight timber batten. Then, bisect this with a horizontal line drawn halfway up the wall with the aid of a spirit level. Make up a gauge rod from a batten stepped off in nominal tile widths – the width of a tile plus a 3 mm (⅛ in) allowance for grouting. Hold this against the two guide lines, and mark off the positions of individual tiles along them.

If you find that the width of tiles needed to fill in around the edges of the wall is impossibly narrow – say, less than 25 mm (1 in) wide – restrike the guide lines in a slightly different position and try again. You should also restrike the guide lines if it looks as if the layout will present other problems around windows or similar obstacles.

Having marked out the wall, decide which method you will use to turn the corners (see overleaf) and continue round the room, checking the tiling arrangement for the remaining walls. Again, if you hit a problem, restrike the original guide lines to overcome it. When you are satisfied, temporarily nail battens round the walls so that their upper edges are level with the bottom edges of the lowest row of whole tiles – either the row above the skirting board, or above an obstacle such as a bath, basin, or worktop. Check that the battens are truly horizontal with a spirit level.

Apply the adhesive to the wall with a notched spreader, covering roughly 1 m² (1 yd²) at a time, and press the tiles firmly into place. Begin with one resting on a batten, its edge against the vertical guide line. Remember to leave a 3mm (⅛ in) gap between tiles for grouting. Some tiles have lugs or chamfered edges which, when butted together, provide this spacing automatically. They are said to be self-spacing. Others must be kept apart with matchsticks or pieces of card.

Continue until all the whole tiles are in place, and allow the adhesive to set. Then remove the support battens, and fill in around the edges with cut tiles. To allow for the fact that the walls may be out of true, measure each end of the gap to be filled, deduct an allowance for grouting, then transfer the measurements to the tile, and join them with a straight line.

Alternatively, use the overlapping method described for cork tiles (see page 48), though this may be difficult unless you have someone there to help you.

When cutting tiles, use a straight-edge as a guide, and run a tile cutter over the surface to score right through the glaze (including any on the tile's edges). Lay the tile face up on a flat surface with a couple of matchsticks immediately beneath the scored line, and press down on both sides of the tile to snap it cleanly in two. More complex shapes – L-shaped tiles, and so on – should be scored in the same way, but the waste should be nibbled out a little at a time with a pair of pincers. By combining the two techniques, you can fit tiles around isolated obstructions such as taps and pipes. Snap the tile in two first, and nibble a notch to accommodate the obstruction.

The problems come when turning corners and tiling into window reveals. On internal corners, you can either work into the angle with two separate whole or cut tiles (in other words treat each wall individually), or you can tile into the corner with a cut tile, and continue on the other wall with the resulting off-cut.

Obviously, the latter gives a better result with patterned tiles.

With external corners, you must tile up to the edge, cutting the tiles so that they finish flush with the second wall. Then, begin covering the second wall with tiles that have glazed edges, overlapping the tiles on the first wall and concealing their edges.

When tiling window reveals, cover the main wall, cutting the tiles to finish flush with the reveal. Tile back from the edge of the reveal, using tiles with glazed edges in the same way as for an external corner. Fill in against the window frame, if necessary, with narrow cut tiles. It's not nearly as difficult as it sounds, but it can prove quite tricky to achieve neat results. The answer really lies in the setting out. If at all possible, pick a tile arrangement that fits symmetrically around each reveal.

Once the wall is tiled completely, leave it overnight, remove any matchstick or card spacers, and apply grout (see page 52). Choose your grout carefully. If the area is constantly wet, select an extra waterproof type. You can even dye the grout a contrasting colour. Buy the special grouting dye. They come in all basic colours. Remember, follow the manufacturer's instructions carefully or you may reduce the grout's effectiveness.

73

*This page:*
*Temporarily nail a batten to the wall to support the bottom row of whole tiles.*
*Begin fixing whole tiles along the batten, working out and up to cover the wall.*
*To cut a tile (below), score through the glaze, including any on the edges, where you want to make the cut.*
*Lay the tile over a couple of matchsticks and press to snap cleanly along the score line.*

*Opposite page:*
*Cut tiles are best dealt with when all the whole tiles are in place around windows (far right), tile the face of the wall first.*
*If L-shaped cut tiles are needed (centre right), score as normal and nibble out the waste with pincers.*
*Tile the window sill, overlapping the wall tiles and working back from the edge.*
*Apply grout generously (below right), working it well into the gaps between tiles.*
*When dry, wash off surplus grout and polish the tiles clean.*

# PLUMBING

## BALL VALVES

Ball valves are a bit like automatic taps. Used in WC cisterns, and in the water storage cisterns in the loft, their job is to open when the water level in the cistern drops, and close once the cistern is full. In most designs, this is achieved using a ball float attached to a lever arm. As the float rises or falls with the water level, the arm slides a piston against the valve seating at the inlet opening, controlling the flow of water into the tank. The first sign of trouble is normally water pouring from the cistern's overflow pipe, indicating that the valve isn't closing when it should.

Begin checking the valve by partially emptying the cistern, and watching the ball float as it refills. If the ball doesn't float, replace it by unscrewing the old one from the lever arm and screwing on the new. Make sure the replacement is the same size or you may create further problems.

Assuming it does float, adjusting its cut-off level should prevent the overflow. Modern plastic valves have a small adjustment screw for this purpose, but with brass valves, you have to bend the lever arm carefully to lower the float in relation to the valve body. Allow the cistern to refill completely, and check that the valve shuts off when the water level is about 25 mm (1 in) below the level of

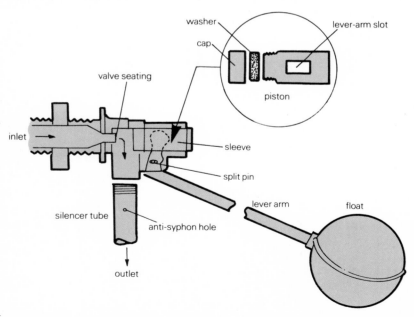

the overflow pipe in the cistern.

If the trouble persists, no matter how much adjustment you make, the valve should be rewashered. Cut off the water supply (see Basic Systems), and pull out the split pin on which the lever arm pivots. By inserting a screwdriver into the slot vacated by the lever arm, you should be able to slide the piston out through the end of the valve body. If an end cap is fitted, unscrew this, taking care not to lose the accompanying washers.

Dismantle the piston by unscrewing the washer retaining cap with a pair of pliers, holding the piston body steady with a screwdriver inserted in the lever-arm slot. Remove the old washer, cut a new one to fit, and reassemble both piston and valve. Restore the water supply, and adjust the lever arm as necessary to achieve the desired water level in the cistern.

If this should fail, dismantle the valve once again and check the condition of the valve seating. Modern valves have plastic valve seat inserts which may be replaced if badly worn. With older valves, however, the seating is an integral part of the inlet, so a complete new ball valve should be fitted.

Another problem is that the valve may fail to open properly, in which case the cistern will be slow to refill. If adjusting the lever arm has no effect, dismantle the valve and clean it out, as it may be blocked. If that doesn't work, check that the valve is right for the job or, in the case of modern dual-purpose valves, has the right plastic seating. Some are designed to be supplied from a high-pressure source, such as the rising main, while others are for a low-pressure supply, such as that from a storage cistern. A low-pressure valve on a high-pressure supply will not close, while a high-pressure valve on a low-pressure supply will not open.

## BASIC SYSTEMS

Even the most basic plumbing job is a lot simpler when you understand how your home's plumbing system is put together (see overleaf).

Water enters your property along a pipe called the rising main, which is connected to the water authority's main via a stop-cock, usually located somewhere in the pavement. This belongs to the authority, so, if you need to turn it off in an emergency, get them to do it. Farther along the rising main, you may find a second underground stop-cock in the garden. This is yours, but often needs a special key to operate it. Therefore, it is more convenient to use the main stop-cock inside the house, close to where the rising main enters the building – generally under the stairs, or under the kitchen sink.

From here, the rising main continues up to the loft, usually with only a single branch off to the kitchen cold-water tap, and empties into a large cold-water storage cistern. This cistern supplies the rest of your water, and normally has at least two pipes leading from it. The first feeds the WCs and bathroom taps; the second puts water into the bottom of the hot-water cylinder. In a modern installation, both outlets will be fitted with gate-valves (a type of stop-cock) close to the cistern.

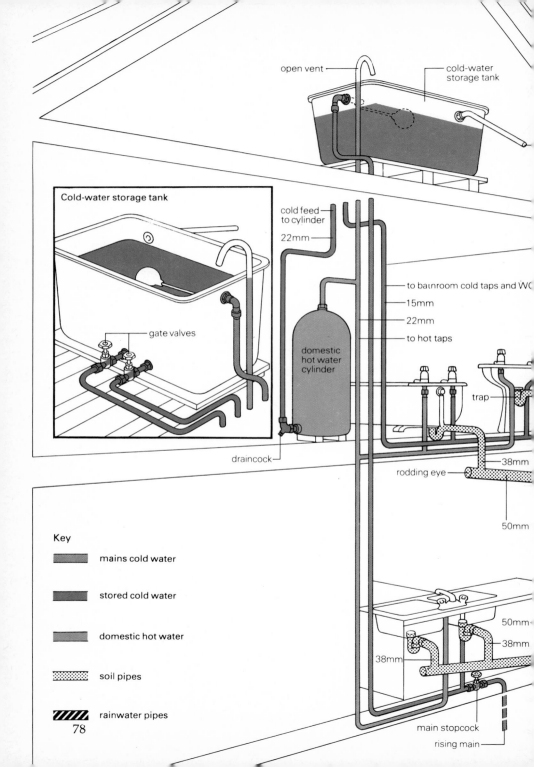

open vent

cold-water storage tank

## Cold-water storage tank

gate valves

cold feed to cylinder

22mm

to bathroom cold taps and WC

15mm

22mm

to hot taps

domestic hot water cylinder

trap

draincock

38mm

rodding eye

50mm

## Key

mains cold water

stored cold water

domestic hot water

soil pipes

rainwater pipes

50mm

38mm

38mm

main stopcock

rising main

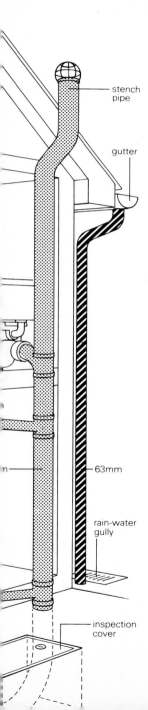

stench
pipe

gutter

63mm

rain-water
gully

inspection
cover

A vent pipe runs back from the top of the hot-water storage cylinder to the top of the cold-water cistern, relieving any pressure build-up in the cylinder. A branch off this supplies all the hot taps in the house.

To complete the installation, any cistern controlled by a ball valve has an overflow pipe which normally discharges outside the house, to avoid any flooding if the cistern overfills. In addition, modern installations have two drain-cocks; one at the bottom of the rising main, the other in the cold feed pipe near to where it enters the hot-water cylinder. These let you drain the pipework to make repairs or alterations, each having a nozzle for connection to a hose that makes it easier to dispose of the water. You may also find extra stop-cocks on branch pipes to washing machines and taps.

Finally, there are ancillary systems: drainage, boiler circuit and central heating. These are dealt with under the relevant headings later in this chapter.

It is important to know how to isolate the various parts of the system. Anything fed directly by the rising main can be cut off at any of the stopcocks on that main. For the rest, if there is a stop-cock or gate-valve on the incoming pipe, turn it off. If there is not, empty the cistern feeding the pipe, and stop it refilling by tying the lever arm in the closed position to a batten braced across the top of the cistern.

*Domestic hot and cold water and waste system: it is important for you to know how this works.*

## CENTRAL HEATING SYSTEMS

There are three main types of central heating system which use water to move heat around the house; they are named according to the size of pipework used. There is large-bore, small-bore and microbore.

Large-bore systems are now obsolete, but you may still find them in old houses. The pipes can be anything up to 50 mm (2 in) in diameter, and the radiators are equally bulky. The reason is that they rely on a combination of gravity and natural convection currents within the circuit to move the hot water around; in fact, they are often called gravity-fed systems.

Small-bore systems use 15, 22 or 28 mm (½, ¾ or 1 in imperial) pipework and slim radiators, relying on an electric pump to circulate the water. They may have single- or two-pipe heating circuits.

In a single-pipe circuit one pipe runs in a loop, carrying hot water from the boiler, through each radiator in turn, and returning it to the boiler for reheating. Towards the end of the loop the water will be rather cool. Although you can compensate for this by progressively increasing the radiator size, or by raising the initial water temperature, it is not a very satisfactory arrangement.

In modern houses, the two-pipe system is more common. Here, one pipe runs from the boiler to each radiator, supplying it with hot water through a short branch pipe. A second, similar pipe run takes the cooled water from each radiator directly to the boiler for reheating.

As its name suggests, the micro-bore system uses very narrow pipes indeed – 6, 8 or 10 mm (¼, 5⁄16 or 3⁄8 in) – allowing the radiator pipe runs to be installed as easily as electric cables. These are connected via manifolds to two larger pipes connected to the boiler. In principle, it is the same as the two-pipe, small-bore system: one circuit distributes hot water; the other removes cooled water. The large pipes correspond to the main pipe runs, and the microbore pipes to the branches off to the radiators. The manifolds are simply a convenient means of joining the two.

## CISTERNS

Since a cistern is nothing more than a container for storing water, there isn't much to go wrong with it. In fact, in a modern installation with its ceramic and PVC cisterns, virtually the only thing that can go wrong is the WC flushing mechanism (see page 93). In older houses, however, the cisterns will probably be metal – galvanized iron for the main cold-water storage cistern; cast iron for WC cisterns – and metal plus water equals rust. So, do inspect old cisterns thoroughly. If they are very rusty, replace them before they leak. This is vital in the case of the main cold-water storage cistern; if it goes, your home will get very wet very quickly.

Before removing the cold-water cistern, turn off the main stop-cock to isolate the ball valve, draining the water by flushing the WC and turning on the bathroom taps. Next, remove the ball valve, disconnect the outlet pipes and overflow, and drag the cistern clear. Almost certainly, it

80

will be too big to go through the loft's trap door, so, unless you really want to saw it up and dispose of it, leave it in a corner of the loft.

The best replacement is a modern PVC cistern with a capacity of 227 litres (50 gallons). This will flex just enough to go through most trap doors, and, once in the loft, should have its base supported on a sheet of 19 mm (¾ in) chipboard – unlike the old cistern it won't tolerate merely resting on the joists.

All that remains is to reconnect the various pipes. You will find this easier if you cut them off some way from the cistern and bridge the gap with new pipework. While you are about it, fit gate valves on the outgoing pipes, and connect the new pipe runs to the cistern with tank connectors seated on polythene washers. You have to cut your own holes for the connectors, using a suitably sized hole saw. Finally, add a close-fitting lid to stop the water becoming contaminated by dead birds, spiders, and other debris.

## DRAINS

The most serious problem you will meet is a blockage in the drain that takes waste from each house in the street to the sewer. This is very unpleasant, and a health risk, so act fast. Begin by tracking down the source of the trouble, asking neighbours to open their manhole covers until you find a flooded chamber next door to an empty one. The blockage will lie between the two, and it is up to the householders concerned to do something about it. If they don't, call in the local council.

If the drain is on your property, it may still be the local authority's responsibility to clear it. If this is not the case, either call in a specialist drain-clearing service, or do the job yourself. The latter is cheaper, but is not to be recommended if you have a weak stomach.

Hire a set of drain rods (semi-flexible canes that screw together) and a selection of drain-clearing heads – at least a plunger and a corkscrew head. Remove the covers from both the flooded and empty inspection chambers, and block the empty chamber's far outlet with a board to stop debris being pushed farther along the system.

Screw a couple of canes together, fit the plunger head, and insert it into the pipe. You will have to feel for the pipe's mouth, but that is better than bailing out the inspection chamber with buckets. Screw on additional canes as necessary and work the plunger along the pipe until it emerges into the dry chamber, carrying the obstruction before it.

If the plunger won't do the job, use the corkscrew head to batter a way through, finishing off with the plunger. If you have to twist the canes for any reason, turn them clockwise or you will unscrew their connections, leaving rods trapped in the drain. Finally, allow the flooded chamber to empty, shovel the debris from both chambers, and use a garden hose to clean the inspection-chamber walls and flush the system through.

You may find that there isn't another chamber between you and the sewer, so the blockage may be in the P-trap which is built into the sewer side of the inspection chamber to keep out sewer gases and rats. Unfortunately, the best way to clear this is to bail the chamber dry and clean out the trap by hand – a nasty job even with rubber gloves. If the trouble persists, you can rod out the pipe to the sewer through the capped rodding eye above the normal outlet. Here, though, it is as well to get the local council to take over, since that part of the drain eventually runs into the street.

damaged section with waterproof tape. Then, slit a length of garden hose down the side and slip it over the pipe, sealing the split with more tape and securing the hose ends with twisted wire or wormdrive clips (bottom). Now turn on the water. This repair should hold until either a plumber arrives, or you cut out and replace the damaged section yourself. If it leaks, partially turn off the relevant stop-cock to reduce the water pressure.

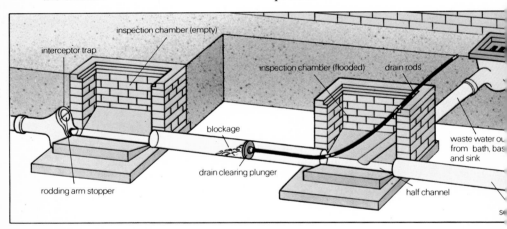

inspection chamber (empty)
interceptor trap
inspection chamber (flooded)
drain rods
blockage
waste water ou
from bath, bas
and sink
drain clearing plunger
rodding arm stopper
half channel

## FROZEN PIPES

Modern copper pipes rarely burst when frozen (though joints may leak), so the first sign of trouble is likely to be a tap running dry. Work back along the pipe run to locate the ice plug – water outlets before it will work; those after it will not. Once you have found it, thaw it out slowly with a hair dryer, an electric fan heater, or a hot-water bottle.

Constantly check for leaks. If one appears, isolate the pipe (see Basic Systems, page 77) and bandage the

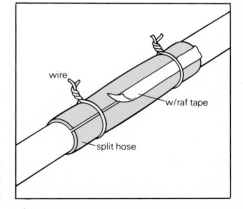

wire
w/raf tape
split hose

Ideally, you shouldn't let the pipes freeze in the first place, and efficient lagging will help in this respect (see page 85).

## GULLIES

Older homes often have open gullies through which sinks, baths, basins and gutters discharge into underground drains, and these frequently become blocked.

Remove the grating, soak it in caustic soda and give it a good scrub. Bail out the standing water from the gulley, and, wearing rubber gloves, scoop out any debris in the trap. This should clear the blockage. If it doesn't, rod the pipe through from the inspection chamber (see Drains), remembering to scoop out whatever the drain rods push into the gully. Finally, flush the system through with plenty of clean water and replace the grating.

## HOT-WATER SYSTEMS

Domestic hot water is supplied from a storage cylinder which, in turn, is fed from the cold-water storage cistern. The manner in which it is heated depends on whether or not your home has a central heating system that relies on hot water to provide warmth.

If you don't have such a system, the water is probably heated inside the cylinder by an electric immersion heater, or elsewhere by a boiler or multi-point gas water heater. Otherwise, the central heating boiler normally does the job (though immersion heaters are often fitted in the cylinder for summer use) using one of two methods.

The simplest method is the direct system (overleaf, left); water in the cylinder actually passes through the boiler to be heated. Unfortunately, the same water also passes through the radiator system at some point. As the system ages, this will produce an adverse effect on the quality of the water that emerges from the taps, and cause corrosion problems.

Modern homes, therefore, tend to have indirect hot-water systems (overleaf, right). Here, the pipework to the taps (the secondary circuit) is completely separate from the primary circuit to the boiler and radiators – the two quantities of water never mix. Instead, water in the secondary circuit takes heat from that in the primary circuit through a heat exchanger – essentially a coiled section of primary circuit – located inside the hot-water cylinder in your home.

Domestic hot-water systems are prone to air locks, but these are easily cured at the kitchen sink. Connect the hot tap to the cold tap with a length of hose held firmly in place with worm-drive clips or twisted wire. Then, turn on both taps fully. The cold water, under mains pressure, will flush any air in the hot water pipes out through the hot-water cylinder's vent pipe.

Accidental venting, due to the water in the cylinder overheatiing, is another possibility – water from the hot taps will be scalding, and warm water will flow from both bathroom cold taps and the cold-water cistern's overflow. The cause is a faulty thermostat (or the lack of a thermostat), either in the boiler or immersion heater. Fit a new one.

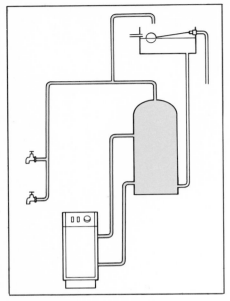
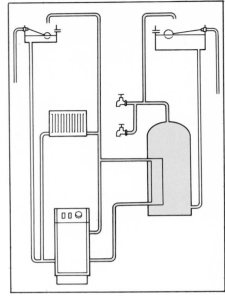

Keeping down the cost of providing hot water is important, particularly with immersion heaters. Make sure you use no more than you need, so fix dripping taps at once, fill basins rather than wash under a running tap, and take a shower in preference to a bath. You should also insulate, fitting the hot-water cylinder with as thick a jacket as possible, and lagging long pipe runs.

As long as the cylinder is well insulated, and there is a good thermostat, it is usually cheaper to leave the immersion heater switched on round the clock. Also, in summer, it is generally cheaper to use an immersion heater than run the central-heating boiler at a reduced level. A dual-element immersion heater can produce real savings. One element heats the top part of the cylinder only, giving enough hot water for most needs. If more is required, say, for a bath, you switch on the second element to heat the rest.

## JOINTS

Although plumbing joint fittings come in all shapes and sizes, there are only five common methods of making a plumbing joint.

For a copper-to-copper joint, the simplest fitting to use is the compression joint. Each end has a brass nut and a copper ring, called an olive, which slip over the pipes to be joined. If the olive has unequal chamfers, the long chamfer runs towards the end of the pipe, which should, incidentally, be cut square and be free from burrs. Each pipe and its olive fit into the joint's body, being retained by screwing on the nut until finger tight. A further 1½ turns of the nut with a spanner will crush the olive between the pipe and joint to provide a waterproof seal. A line marked on the nut and on the joint body will aid in counting the number of turns, and you can prevent the joint body turning by simultaneously tightening the nut at the other end, or by gripping the joint with a wrench. If necessary, the nut may be tightened slightly more to achieve a seal, but take care not to over-tighten it.

Unfortunately, compression joints can work out too expensive for large jobs, so use ready-soldered capillary joints. Again, cut the pipe ends square and remove any burrs with a file. Clean the pipe and the inside of the fitting with wire wool (top left, page 86) until bright, and mark the position of the joint on the pipe (top right, page 86). Smear a little soldering flux on both surfaces (bottom left, page 86). Push the pipes hard into the joint, and apply a blowlamp flame, shielding whatever is behind the pipe with a piece of asbestos (bottom right, page 86). When a ring of molten solder appears around the end of the fitting, remove the flame and leave the joint to cool.

Copper-to-iron connections are available for joining pipes to taps and so on. The copper end of the fitting uses either a compression or capillary joint. The iron end may have either a threaded socket that screws over a threaded tail-pipe, or a spigot and retaining nut which squeezes a fibre washer against the end of the tail-pipe. In either case, wrap the tail-pipe in PTFE tape, or coat it in plumber's jointing compound, and screw on the fitting or retaining nut with a spanner.

As for other materials, square pipe ends are essential for good joints in plastic pipework. A paper collar round the cut line will help when cutting large-diameter pipes. For joints containing a rubber D-ring seal, coat the pipe and interior of the fitting with a special lubricant, push them together, then withdraw the pipe by about 3 mm (⅛ in) to allow for expansion. With solvent-welded joints, clean the pipe and joint interior with glasspaper before brushing on a generous coat of special solvent adhesive (top right, page 87). Push the pipe home, working quickly, as the adhesive bonds rapidly.

## LAGGING

Lagging is insulation fitted to water pipes and tanks to stop them freezing. It should be used on all outdoor plumbing, all plumbing in the loft, and on any pipes run against external walls.

There are two types of lagging for pipes. Glassfibre bandage is wound around the pipe (wear gloves) and secured at intervals with string, or sticky tape (bottom left, page 87). Foam plastic, on the other hand, comes as a tube split along its length. Slip it over the pipe and seal splits and joints with adhesive tape (bottom right, page 87).

Insulation may be improvised for water tanks. Consider enclosing the tank in glassfibre blanket, or in a box made of polystyrene slabs taped together. Alternatively, construct a

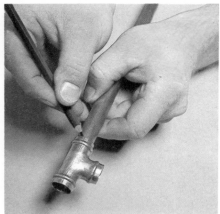

*Top left: Clean the pipe and fitting until bright using wire wool.*

*Bottom left: Coat the inside of the fitting and pipe end with flux.*

*Top right: Slip the fitting on to the pipe and mark its position in pencil.*

*Bottom right: Heat the joint until solder appears round the ends of the fitting.*

hardboard case around the tank and fill it with loose-fill loft insulation; don't forget the lid.

## OVERFLOWS

Any cistern filled by a ball valve has an overflow warning pipe about 25 mm (1 in) above normal water level. If the valve is faulty and won't turn off, the pipe drains off surplus water, discharging it outside the house, or into a sink or bath. This stops the cistern spilling over and flooding your home.

*Fit large plastic pipes with a paper collar to help you cut the end square.*

*Coat the surfaces to be joined with adhesive and assemble the joint.*

## PIPES

There are two basic kinds of pipe: the kind that supplies water to fittings, and the kind that carries it away. However, you will find a wide variety of sizes and materials within each category.

In old installations, water-carrying pipes may be of lead, or galvanized iron, and work on these is best left to a plumber. More modern homes will have copper pipes (correctly called copper tubing), at least for hot water. A few use plastic for the cold-water

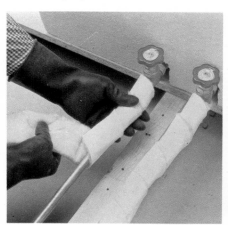

*One way to lag pipes is to wrap them in glass fibre bandage.*

*Another is to use split foam plastic tubes secured with adhesive tape.*

runs, but this is frowned on by the more conservative water authorities.

If possible, match the existing material when making replacements or alterations, but be sure to use the correct size for the job. For rising mains, branches to WCs, and branches to sink and basin taps, use 15 mm (equivalent to ½ in imperial pipe). However, because metric pipe sizes refer to external diameter and imperial sizes refer to the bore, metric and imperial pipes are not exactly the same. Hot and cold water runs that are not mains fed, and branches to bath taps, should be 22 mm (or ¾ in imperial). This will also serve for the feed from the cold-water storage cistern to the hot-water cylinder, though 28 mm (1 in equivalent) is probably better. Note that the metric/imperial sizes are rough equivalents only. Old imperial and modern metric pipes have fractionally different diameters, making the two difficult to join. A special olive is needed when using compression fittings; feed in extra solder with capillary fittings.

The second category of pipe includes waste pipes, soil pipes, and overflows. In the past, these were made of lead, cast iron, stainless steel and other materials. Today, almost all are plastic because it's cheap, light, and very easy to use. When buying, make sure you get the right size, and the right kind of plastic for the job.

Sizing is reasonably straightforward. Soil pipes are usually 110 or 160 mm (4 or 6 in in imperial) in diameter; bath and sink wastes, 40 mm (1½ in); hand basin wastes, 32 mm (1¼ in); and overflows 22 mm (¾ in).

Rigid PVC is the norm for soil pipes, and polypropylene for waste pipes.

## SOIL SYSTEMS

In most pre-war houses, the soil pipe carrying the waste from the WC was kept separate from all other waste pipes, the latter often discharging into open gullies and hoppers built into the guttering system. As an extra precaution against 'foul air' getting into the house from the drains, as much of the pipework as possible was run down the outside of the house, the WC soil pipe being extended above the eaves to ventilate the underground drains. This is called a two-pipe system.

In modern homes, however, a single soil stack runs inside the house with branches to the WCs, baths, sinks, and basins. The only similarity with the earlier system is that the stack continues up above the roof for ventilation.

Another design you may come across is the twin-stack system; not to be confused with the two-pipe system. Actually, this is a single-stack layout with a matching parallel system of vent pipes to prevent water being sucked out of the various waste traps. The latter is a constant risk in single-stack systems, and can only be avoided by careful design. So, do get expert advice before altering or adding to this type of soil system.

## TAPS

Although modern taps may look very different from their old-fashioned counterparts, most of the faults remain the same. The commonest is dripping, and the cure is simple – fit

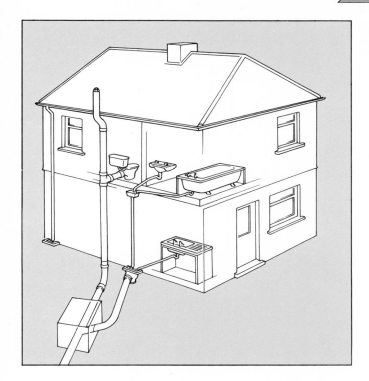

a new washer to the dripping tap.

Isolate the tap, and turn it on until it runs dry. If it is of the conventional pillar type, protect the shield or cover with thick fabric tape, and unscrew it with a wrench to expose the head – the body of the tap containing all the moving parts. Unscrew this with a spanner fitted over the hexagonal moulding near the base. It will be stiff, so grip the tap firmly to stop it turning and damaging the sink or basin. If there isn't room for the spanner beneath the shield, remove the tap handle by loosening the retaining screw at the side and tapping it upwards with a hammer. Then, lift off the shield.

You'll find the jumper, which carries the washer, beneath the tap head, either stuck to the latter or in the tap base. Having pulled this out, grip its spindle with a pair of pliers, remove the small washer retaining nut, and the old washer. Fit a new washer and reassemble the tap. Finally, restore the water supply, and turn off the tap once water is flowing freely.

Modern pillar taps are tackled in more or less the same way. The only difference is that the shrouded head – the bit you turn to work the tap – doubles as both handle and shield cover. How you remove it depends on the make of tap, but in most cases,

*Pillar tap*

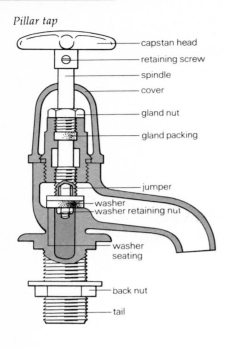

- capstan head
- retaining screw
- spindle
- cover
- gland nut
- gland packing
- jumper
- washer
- washer retaining nut
- washer seating
- back nut
- tail

*Supatap*

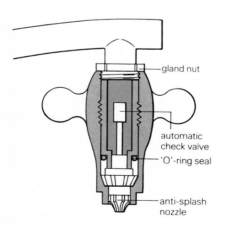

- gland nut
- automatic check valve
- 'O'-ring seal
- anti-splash nozzle

*Shrouded-head tap*

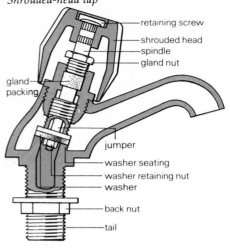

- retaining screw
- shrouded head
- spindle
- gland nut
- gland packing
- jumper
- washer seating
- washer retaining nut
- washer
- back nut
- tail

prising off the small plastic 'Hot' or 'Cold' button will reveal a retaining screw. Remove this, and pull off the head.

Supataps require a different approach, and there is no need to turn off the water supply. Turn on the tap slightly, and loosen the locking nut with a spanner. Continue turning the tap until the nozzle comes away, and a check valve cuts off the water. Tap the end of the nozzle on a hard surface to release its anti-splash device, prising off the combined jumper/washer to replace it. Reefit the anti-splash device, screw the nozzle back on until the tap is almost turned off, then retighten the lock nut. Turn off the tap fully.

Finally, there are stop-taps, or stop-cocks. These work in exactly the same way as pillar taps, but, because they are used so infrequently, it's rare for them to require rewashering. Their most common fault is due solely to the fact that they are not used very often; they become so stiff through disuse, that you cannot turn them off. This could be disastrous if you need to cut off the water supply in an emergency, so it pays to service stop taps regularly.

Turn them on and off three or four times a year. With stiff taps, apply a little penetrating oil around the spindle, leave it to soak in for a few hours, then try again. If it still refuses to budge, try using a wrench to get extra leverage, but be careful not to break off the spindle. If the stop-tap is that rigid, however, you would do better to leave it until you can fit a new one.

## TRAPS

All waste pipes, including underground drains, open gullies and WC pipes, are fitted with traps holding pockets of water which stop unpleasant drain smells finding their way back up the pipes. Those most likely to give trouble are incorporated in bath, basin and sink waste pipes. Although they come in many different types (overleaf), including some with integral overflows, they are all prone to blockage. Fortunately, this is not serious.

Most modern plastic traps can be removed by undoing the large retaining nuts, and flushed through to clear any blockage. Have a bucket handy to catch any water in the sink, as it will pour out when you take the trap away. Bottle traps are even less of a problem; just unscrew the lower part of the bottle. The only types that may prove difficult are those with rodding eyes – most old-fashioned

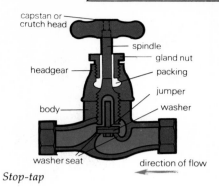
*Stop-tap*

traps, and some modern bath traps. Unless it is possible to remove this trap completely, all you can do is remove the rodding eye, and try to poke out the obstruction with a piece of wire.

Blockages are not the only problem, however. If the drainage system is badly designed, the water in the trap may be sucked out. The reasons for this are complicated, but, in most cases, there is a simple solution – fit a special anti-siphon trap. This should maintain its seal, no matter what.

There is just one other problem you may encounter where stop-taps are concerned, and that is a loss of water pressure on taps fed from a cold-water storage cistern. What has that to do with stop-taps? Well, the stop-tap on the cistern's outlet pipes could be holding the water back.

The ordinary sort of stop-tap, normally made from brass and with a simple crutch or capstan handle, is primarily designed for high-pressure pipes such as the rising main. For the low-pressure pipes – those supplied from a cistern – a special stop-tap called a gate valve should be used. This is most easily recognized by the

91

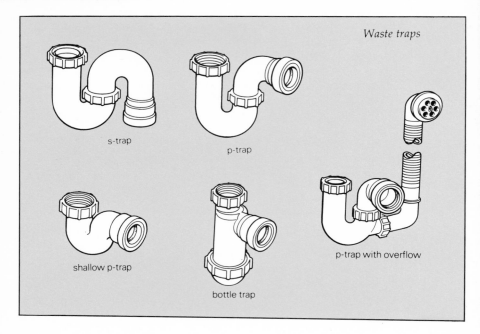

*Waste traps*

s-trap

p-trap

shallow p-trap

bottle trap

p-trap with overflow

vaguely flower-shaped wheel-style handle.

## WASHING MACHINES

To reap the full benefits of an automatic washing machine, you should connect it permanently to the hot and/or cold water supply (machines vary in this respect), as well as to the waste system. This is not difficult; in fact the necessary bits and pieces, with instructions, are available as a kit. However, there are a few points to watch.

Firstly, the branch pipes taking water to the machine should be fitted with stop-taps so the machine can be isolated quickly in an emergency. Secondly, most kits assume the machine will go in the kitchen, and will draw its cold-water supply from

the rising main. The local water authority may object to this because of the risk of contaminating drinking water, so you may have to run a new cold-water supply from the cold-water storage cistern. In this case, it is sensible to check with the machine's manufacturer that this will give enough water pressure for the machine to work.

Finally, the waste pipe is unusual. It consists of a P-trap and a 40 mm (1½ in) pipe leading to the discharge point (either a boss connection to a soil stack, or a stand pipe over an open gully). On the machine side of the trap, a second 40 mm (1½ in) pipe is fixed vertically to the wall with the machine's waste hose pushed into its end so the water does not siphon back into the machine.

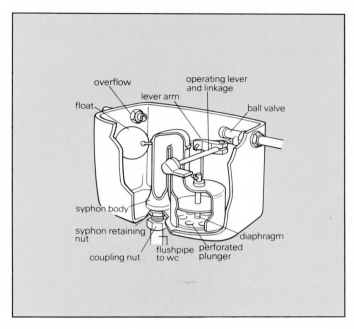

## WATER AUTHORITIES & BY-LAWS

In recent years, water authorities have begun to exercise much tighter control over the sort of new plumbing installations they will permit. If you wish to alter your home's plumbing in any way, you must give the local authority at least seven days' notice of your intentions. They will tell you if they approve of your proposals, and will check that the work has been done properly. If you fail to inform them, you could be liable for a heavy fine.

## WATER CLOSETS

Blockages apart, the main problem with WCs is that their cisterns (opposite, right) sometimes fail to flush. Asssuming there is enough water in the cistern – if there is not, check the ball valve – the trouble lies with the flap valve inside the siphon bell.

To gain access to the flap valve, tie the ball-valve float arm in the closed position, and bale out the water from the cistern. Disconnect the flush pipe by undoing its retaining nut, and have a bucket standing by to catch any water left in the cistern. Undo the large nut above the flush pipe and lift out the siphon mechanism – in some models additional bolts inside the cistern must also be removed to free it.

Remove the old flap valve – a round rubber diaphragm – and fit a new one. If you cannot find a replacement of the right size, buy a larger one, cutting it down with scissors so that it fits snugly.

# ELECTRICS

## CABLES & FLEXES

Cables and flexes are the backbone of any electrical installation. So, if your house electrics are to be safe and efficient, you must choose the right type for the job.

The difference between cables and flexes is simple. Cables form the fixed wiring – that is the wiring taking power to socket outlets, ceiling roses, and so on; flexes link appliances and light fittings to the fixed wiring.

Most indoor fixed wiring is 2-core and earth, PVC sheathed and insulated cable. This has three copper wires (the cores): a bare earth wire; a red PVC insulated live wire; and a black PVC insulated neutral wire. All are enclosed in a flattened PVC shea-

thing. Sizes, given as the area in square millimetres of each core's cross-section, vary according to the rating of the circuit in which the cable is to be used – the thicker the core, the more electricity it can carry. Common sizes are 2.5 mm$^2$ for ring circuits; 4 or 6 mm$^2$ for cooker circuits; and 1.0 or 1.5 mm$^2$ for lighting circuits.

You may also find cable with three insulated cores (colour coded red, blue and yellow) plus a bare earth. It is used only in two-way switching circuits (see page 105).

Flexes come in a greater variety, but, basically, two-core types are for lights and double-insulated appliances; three-core types for all other appliances, and for lights that need

1    2    3    4    5    6    7    8

earthing. Sizes range from 0.5 mm² for small lights, up to 4 mm² for very large appliances. Some are kink resistant, or heat resistant. The only time you need buy flex is when an old flex has worn out, and all you need do is buy the same again.

Finally, note that flexes have a different colour coding to cables: brown for live, blue for neutral, and green/yellow for earth.

## CABLE RUNNING

In most electrical jobs, running new cables involves more time and effort than any other task, but forward planning will often reduce the amount of work involved.

First, decide if the cables are to be surface-mounted or concealed. The latter is more difficult, but gives very neat results because all the cables are hidden above ceilings, under floors, or within walls. Concealed wiring is the norm for domestic installations; surface wiring is reserved for situations where looks don't matter (inside garages, for example), or where concealed wiring is impractical.

When installing surface wiring, try to run the cables just above skirting boards, around architraves, in the corners of the room, and in the angle between walls and ceiling. This will make it less obvious. Either pin it in place with cable clips, hammered into the surface at about 150 mm (6 in) intervals, or feed it through plastic mini trunking. The latter consists of a cable trough with a clip-on cover, and is fixed to the wall with screws and wall plugs.

Concealed wiring methods vary according to the surface. In the loft and beneath a suspended ground floor, the cables can be laid between or across the joists, as appropriate. If you can reach them, clip them into place. For all other suspended timber floors, lift the floorboards and feed the cables between the joists, or pass them through holes drilled at least 50 mm (2 in) from the top edge of each joist.

Cables can be run inside a stud partition wall by boring a hole in the top and dropping the cable through the void. For all other walls, use a club hammer and cold chisel to chop

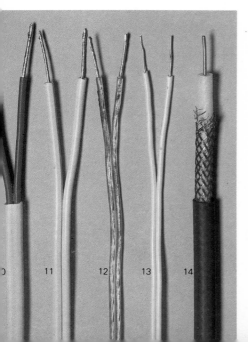

*The basic cables and flexes used in electrical installation –*
*1 to 4: Twin core and earth PVC sheathed and insulated cables;*
*5: 3-core and earth PVC sheathed and insulated cable;*
*6 to 8: 3-core round flexes;*
*9-13: Twin-core flexes;*
*14: Co-axial television aerial cables.*

out a channel in the plaster. Run the cable through a length of plastic conduit, mounted in the channel, and cover it with fresh plaster. All cables buried in this way should run vertically to their fittings. This is where people expect them to be, so there is less chance of drilling into them by accident.

## CLOSE-FITTING LIGHTS

A close-fitting light is one that is mounted hard against the wall or ceiling, thus doing away with pendant flexes, etc. Its main value is in situations where headroom is limited, or in bathrooms where pendant light fittings are regarded as unsafe. The latter is because people have had accidents changing light bulbs whilst standing on the edge of the bath. A close-fitting light forces you to do the job properly, that is while standing on a step ladder.

Don't confuse close-fitting lights with enclosed light fittings, though. The fact that many close-fitting kitchen and bathroom lights are also enclosed is because enclosed lights are good at keeping out dirt and steam. However, the two terms are not synonymous.

## CONSUMER UNITS

The consumer unit (often referred to as the fuse box) is simply a central distribution point, receiving power from the mains via the electricity meter, and making it available to the various lighting and power circuits in your home. All circuit cable runs begin at the consumer unit.

All consumer units have a mains switch to isolate the whole of your home's electrical installation, plus fuseways (see Fuses, page 98) for the individual circuits. Each circuit cable's live conductor is connected to the appropriate fuseway, while its neutral and earth conductors are connected to common earth and neutral terminal blocks. Note that the consumer unit's earth terminal is not 'the earth'; it is merely a convenient device for bringing all circuit earth conductors together, allowing a single cable to be run from the consumer unit to whatever earthing device the system uses (see Earthing).

## DIMMER SWITCHES

A dimmer switch is a device that not only switches lights on and off, but also controls their intensity. As well as making your lighting a good deal more versatile, it offers the very real, practical advantages of saving power, and extending the life of the light bulbs it controls. However, it will not work with fluorescent lights.

Various types of dimmer switch are available; some have built-in fuses to protect the switch's electronics; some have separate switches which allow the lights to be turned on and off at a pre-set lighting level. All are very easy to fit in place of existing one-way light switches.

First, you must turn off the power at the consumer unit, and remove the screws from the switch face plate, so that you can ease the switch from the wall. Behind it, you should find a metal or plastic box containing a 2-core and earth cable. The earth conductor (which should be fitted with green, or green and yellow, PVC sleeving) will be connected to a terminal on the box and can be left. The other two conductors, however, should be disconnected from the switch terminals, and the switch removed.

Connect the two conductors to the dimmer switch – one to the terminal marked VL; the other to the terminal marked L2. It shouldn't matter which way round they go; although colour coded black and red, both cables in switch drops are technically live. Finally, screw the dimmer to its box and restore the power.

## EARTHING

The earthing in an electrical system acts like a safety valve. If anything goes wrong, it provides the electricity with an easy escape route, resulting, indirectly, in a blown fuse which safely cuts off the power to the faulty circuit. Without the earth, the power might well choose a person touching, say, a faulty appliance as its escape route.

As already mentioned, all cables used in circuit wiring have earth conductors which are connected to the earth terminals of the various fittings in the system, linking them to the earthing block in the consumer unit. If required, any appliance or light can be earthed simply by connecting its earth wire to that in the cable. This may be done directly through the outlet's earth terminal, or indirectly through the earth pin in a three-pin plug.

In addition, other metal objects around the home – certainly water mains, and gas pipes – are linked to the earth via earthing clamps and independently run 6 mm$^2$ green/yellow PVC-insulated, single-core cable. This is called crossbonding, and is designed to earth the gas and plumbing systems; NOT to use the gas and water pipes as an earth. Once common practice, the latter is dangerous.

Having connected everything to the consumer unit's earth terminal block, connect the block to the earthing terminal near the meter, or on the sheathing of the main service cable bringing power into the house.

There are just two snags with the system. Firstly, it can be rather slow to react to faults, so it is still possible to get a nasty shock from a faulty appliance. Secondly, there are certain faults to which it doesn't react at all. In some circumstances, if these go undetected, they can start fires.

The solution to these problems is to install a device that will turn off the power immediately it detects the slightest amount of electricity in the earthing system – a current-operated, earth leakage circuit breaker (ELCB for short). Modern versions are extremely sensitive, requiring as little as 30 mA (30 thousandths of an amp) to trip, as opposed to the 1 or 1½ amps needed by older types.

You may come across another type of ELCB which is voltage operated. This detects faults by monitoring the live and neutral conductors. Although more sensitive than old current-operated types, it is, however, prone to accidental tripping, and is no longer widely available.

## FUSED CONNECTION UNITS

A fused connection unit does the job of both power socket and plug, connecting portable appliances to the

*Fused connection unit*

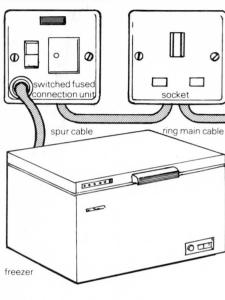

switched fused connection unit

socket

spur cable

ring main cable

freezer

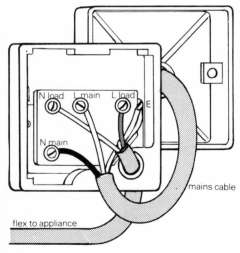

N load   L main   L load

E

N main

mains cable

flex to appliance

fixed wiring permanently. This has clear advantages for something like a freezer, where accidental disconnection would be disastrous. However, the unit is also used to provide power in a bathroom – ordinary sockets are not allowed here – and to 'down grade' ring-circuit spurs to wall lights, and clocks.

Replacing an existing single power socket with a fused connection unit is simple. Turn off the power at the consumer unit, undo the screws in the socket's face plate, and ease it away so you can disconnect it. Feed the appliance flex into the connection unit, connecting the blue wire to the N LOAD terminal, the brown to the L LOAD and the green/yellow wire to the earth. Next, connect the existing circuit cables, and there may be up to three: red to L MAIN, black to N MAIN, and the bare copper earth wire (insulated with green or green/yellow sleeving) to the earth.

If there is no suitable existing socket, install the unit at the end of a spur (see page 105).

## FLUORESCENT LIGHTS

When replacing a conventional pendant light with a fluorescent light, turn off the power at the consumer unit, remove the cover from the ceiling rose, mark each wire with a numbered label, and carefully note which is connected to which. Disconnect the rose. Then, reconnect the wires, exactly as before, in a four-terminal joint box screwed to the side of a joist, replacing the pendant flex with a length of 1.5 mm$^2$ 2-core and earth cable. Remember to insulate its earth conductor with green/yellow PVC

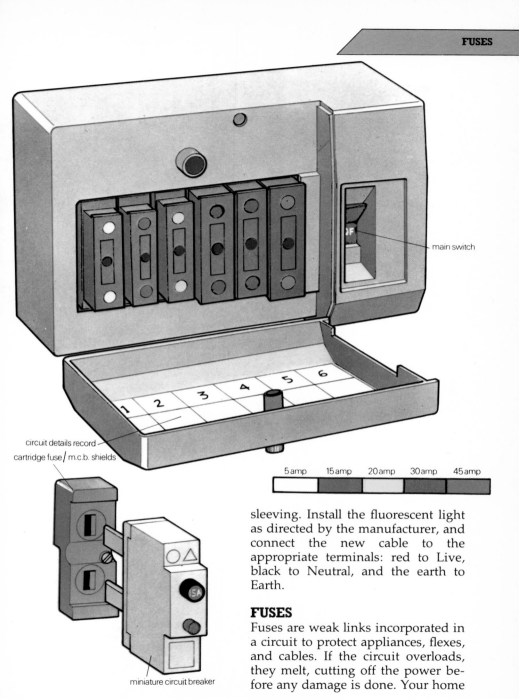

main switch

circuit details record

cartridge fuse / m.c.b. shields

| 5 amp | 15 amp | 20 amp | 30 amp | 45 amp |
|---|---|---|---|---|

miniature circuit breaker

sleeving. Install the fluorescent light as directed by the manufacturer, and connect the new cable to the appropriate terminals: red to Live, black to Neutral, and the earth to Earth.

## FUSES

Fuses are weak links incorporated in a circuit to protect appliances, flexes, and cables. If the circuit overloads, they melt, cutting off the power before any damage is done. Your home will have two sets: those in plugs and fused connection units, and those in the consumer unit.

The former are simple replaceable cartridges that come in two standard ratings: 3 amp for appliances up to 720 watts, and 13 amp for everything else.

Circuit fuses may be either cartridges or bare fuse wire, carried in holders that plug into the consumer unit's fuseways (page 99, above right). Alternatively, miniature circuit breakers (MCBs) may be used (page 99, left). These are more sensitive, and more convenient – when they blow, you merely push a button to reset them. The most common ratings for circuit fuses and MCBs are 5 amp (colour coded white) for lighting, and 30 amp (red) for ring circuits. For cookers, immersion heaters, and radial power circuits, 15 amp (blue), 20 amp (yellow), and 45 amp (green) fuses are available.

## JOINT BOXES

Although most wiring accessories (power sockets, etc.) will accommodate all the cable connections needed to make up a circuit, occasionally joints are needed elsewhere, using joint (or junction) boxes. The most common type is a round plastic box, containing three or four terminals (for use in power and lighting circuits respectively). Its lid, retained by a screw, rotates to open or close cable entry slots in the sides.

## LIGHTING & POWER CIRCUITS

Before attempting any electrical work, you should understand how

*Lighting circuit with junction box and loop-in method.*

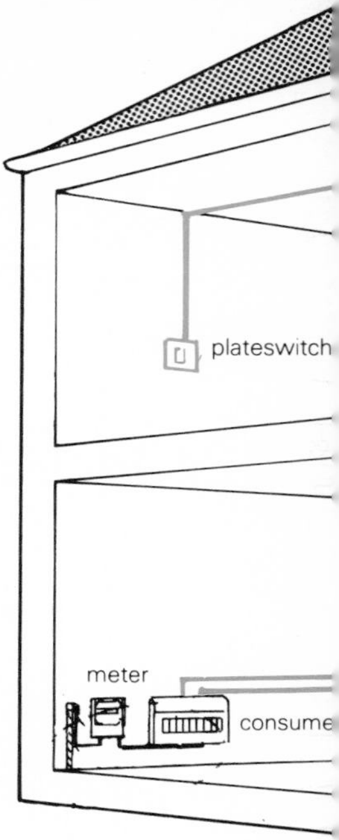

plateswitch

meter

consume

immersion heater

socket

Upstairs ring main

cooker control unit

consumer

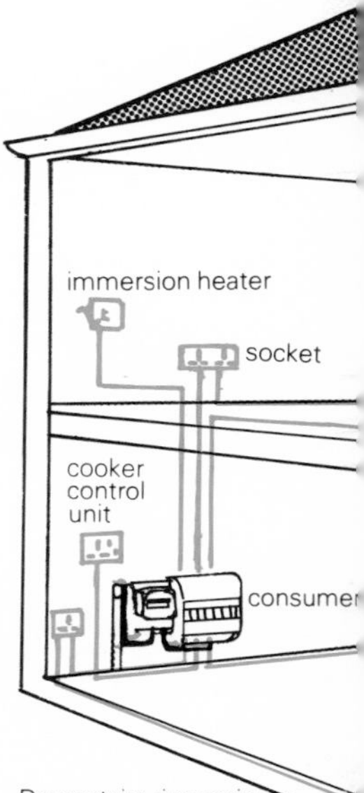

Downstairs ring main

100

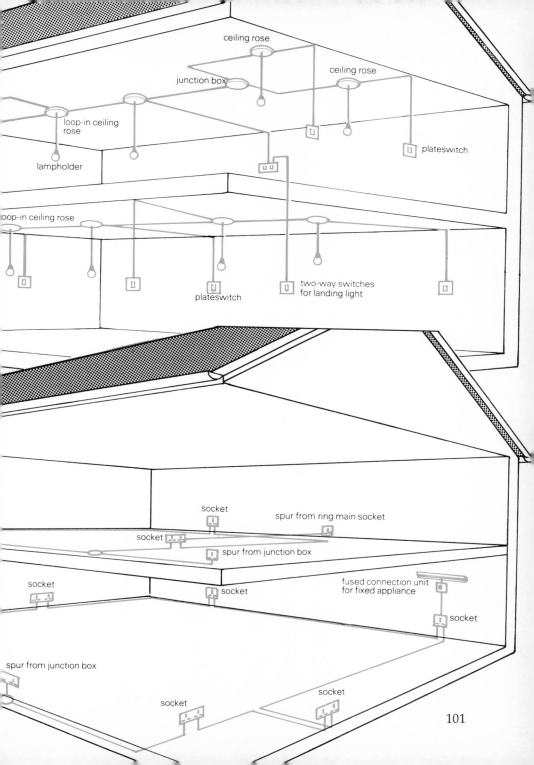

ceiling rose

junction box

ceiling rose

loop-in ceiling
rose

plateswitch

lampholder

oop-in ceiling rose

plateswitch

two-way switches
for landing light

socket

spur from ring main socket

socket

spur from junction box

socket

socket

fused connection unit
for fixed appliance

socket

spur from junction box

socket

socket

101

the various circuits are put together. The most common layouts for both power and lighting circuits are shown on page 101.

Lighting circuits may be run using the loop-in method or the joint-box method; often a combination of the two is used. In the loop-in system, a cable carries power from the consumer unit through a series of loop-in ceiling roses, terminating at the last rose in the circuit. At each rose, power is drawn off around a loop made up of the switch drop cable and the pendant light flex. It passes through the switch, back to the rose,

**Loop-in method.**

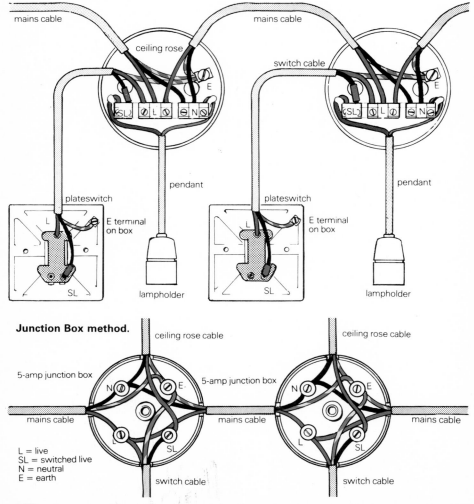

**Junction Box method.**

L = live
SL = switched live
N = neutral
E = earth

down to the light, and up again to the rose's neutral terminal (top).

The joint-box system (bottom) achieves the same looping in a slightly different way. Here, the cable from the consumer unit passes through a series of joint boxes. At each box, power is drawn off along the cable to the switch, returned to the joint box, and sent down another cable to the light. The connections to the bulb holder flex are made within a simple two-terminal ceiling rose, or, in the case of a wall light, within the light's mounting box.

Whichever method is used, most homes will have at least two lighting circuits, so that if a fuse blows, you will not be in total darkness. Normally, each supplies a maximum of eight light fittings throughout the house.

Power circuits also come in two forms. Most socket outlets and fixed appliances are fed directly from a ring circuit, or from a spur off it; the basic ring is a cable run from the consumer unit, through each socket outlet (below) in turn, and back to the consumer unit to be connected to the fuseway at which it began. This allows one ring circuit, in the average home, to carry as many sockets as needed. However, most homes will have two ring circuits, for the same reason as there are two lighting circuits.

The alternative is the radial circuit, which is run like a ring except that it doesn't return to the consumer unit. This limits its flexibility, and now it

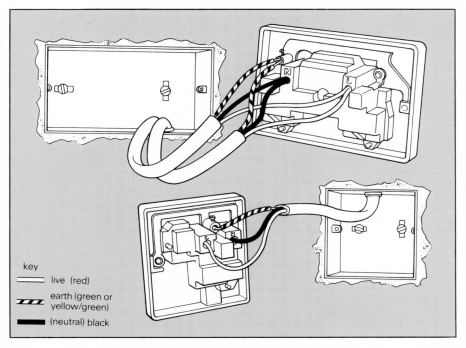

key

—————— live (red)

▰▰▰ earth (green or yellow/green)

━━━━ (neutral) black

103

is rarely used to feed power sockets. You will find it, though, taking power to specific appliances such as cookers and immersion heaters – appliances which are too powerful for a normal ring circuit.

## REWIRING

If the electrical installation in your home is old and, in particular, the cables are not PVC sheathed and insulated, you should not attempt partial modernization. Have the entire system stripped and rewired to modern standards. Rewiring may also be needed if PVC cables are more than 15 years old. Rather than wait until things begin to go wrong, check the cables for cracking or brittleness.

If you are reasonably handy, reasonably intelligent, and are prepared to do a lot of research, you should be able to manage the rewiring yourself. However, it's a mammoth project, so consider getting a qualified electrician to put in the new earth, consumer unit, and main circuits. Then you can modify these to meet your particular needs at leisure.

## SAFETY & REGULATIONS

Electrical work isn't as difficult or dangerous as you might think, but, the fact remains, electricity can kill. Therefore, it must be treated with respect and commonsense.

Before attempting any electrical work, turn off the power at the consumer unit, and keep it off until you have finished. If you need power in the meantime (say, for an electric drill), isolate the circuit on which you will be working by switching off

its MCB or by pulling out its fuse holder.

Follow whatever instructions you are working to, to the letter. If you cannot understand them, or if they don't seem to fit in with the reality of the situation, don't experiment. Stop what you are doing, and call in a qualified electrician.

Remember, although you don't need permission to carry out electrical work, the work you do must comply with the IEE (Institute of Electrical Engineers) Wiring Regulations, and must be checked by your local electricity board.

## SOCKET INSTALLATION

One of the most useful techniques you can master is that of installing a flush-mounted power socket, for you can adapt it to fitting light switches, fused connection units, and so on. Naturally, the wiring is different in each case.

Take a metal mounting box of the correct size for the socket, hold it against the wall so it is level, and draw round it in pencil. Using an electric drill and masonry bit, bore holes on the waste side of the outline, making each hole as close to its neighbour as possible. Chop out the masonry inside the outline with a club hammer and cold chisel, leaving a hole just deep enough to take the mounting box. Fix the latter in place with screws driven into wall plugs.

Run the required cables to the box, passing them through one of its knock-out holes, fitted with a rubber grommet. Having left about 150 mm (6 in) of cable protruding from the box, make good the wall's plaster.

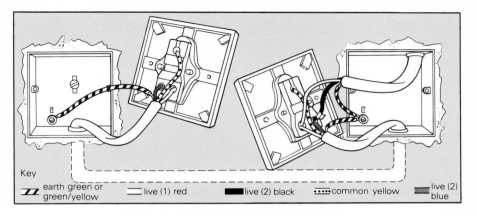

Key

⚡ earth green or green/yellow ▭ live (1) red ■ live (2) black ▦▦ common yellow ▨ live (2) blue

Finally, strip off the cable's outer sheathing with a sharp knife – remove no more than is necessary, and take care not to cut into the individual insulation of each wire – bare the ends of the wires, and make the connections as required (see Lighting and Power Circuits, page 100). Screw the socket face plate securely to the box.

## SPURS

A spur is basically a branch off a ring circuit. You are allowed as many spurs as there are socket outlets on the ring, but each spur may feed only one outlet: a single socket, a fused connection unit, or a double socket.

To install a spur, fit the new outlet in the required position (see Lighting & Power Circuits for the wiring) and run a length of 2.5 mm$^2$ 2-core and earth from it to where you intend making the connection with the ring. An existing power socket is often simplest, but you can break into the ring-circuit cables at any point with a three-terminal joint box.

Screw this to the side of a joist under the floor, cut the ring cable and connect both red wires to one terminal, both black wires to another, and the earth wires (fitted with green/yellow sleeving) to the third.

Finally, connect the spur cable wires to the three terminals in the same way.

## TWO-WAY SWITCHING

Two-way switching allows you to turn a light on and off at either one of two switches. In the main, it is used to control stairwell lights from upstairs as well as downstairs, but it can also be equally useful in rooms with two doors, or in bedrooms where it can save you getting out of bed to operate the light switch. It is quite simple to install.

To convert to two-way switching, install a two-way switch at the second switching position, and run a 3-core and earth cable to the existing switch. Here, replace the old switch with a new two-way unit, and connect up to the existing cable as shown above.

105

# WOODWORKING

## ABRASIVES

The most common, and the cheapest, abrasive is glasspaper (often incorrectly called sandpaper). It can be used on most relatively soft materials (wood, paint, etc.), but it clogs easily, wears out quickly, and removes waste rather slowly.

A more-durable, faster-cutting alternative for work on timber is garnet paper. Unfortunately, since it is made from the semi-precious stone of that name, it is rather expensive, and not widely available.

Aluminium oxide, a man-made abrasive, is probably a better bet, but this is not cheap either. However, it has a very long working life, and removes material quickly. What's more, it is versatile, coping with wood, paint, and even metal.

Silicon carbide is another artificial abrasive worth considering. It gives excellent results on metal, paint, and other finishes, and can be used either dry or dipped in water (hence 'wet and dry', its alternative name) to reduce clogging and lengthen its life. It should not be used on wood, though.

Emery is not suitable for use on wood, either. This slow-cutting, short-lived abrasive is designed solely for polishing metal.

Finally, there is tungsten carbide. Available only on a metal backing for use with power tools, it is extremely hard, extremely sharp, and will cope with almost any material. It is also extremely expensive.

Having chosen the type of abrasive you need, consider the form it comes in, and the grade. With the exception of tungsten carbide, all are available in standard sheets for hand use, as well as in smaller sheets for orbital sanders, or discs for disc sanders. Normally, they are paper-backed, but glass and emery can be obtained with a cloth backing as well.

Choosing a grade – the degree of coarseness – is more complicated. Although traditional abrasives, such as glasspaper, come in grades with descriptive names (coarse, medium, fine, etc.). man-made abrasives tend

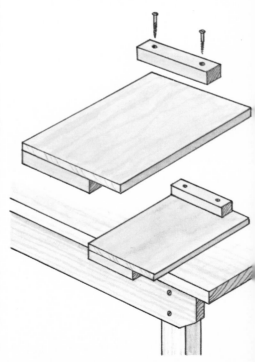

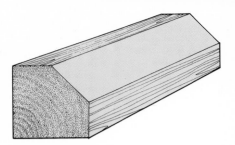

to use a system of grade numbers, and the numbering varies from one abrasive to another. The best advice, therefore, is to run your fingers over the surface of the sheet to see if it is what you want.

## ADHESIVES

Modern adhesives are far superior to old-fashioned glues. They are cleaner, stronger, much more convenient and, in most cases, quicker to bond. However, most modern adhesives will refuse to stick unless the surfaces being bonded are smooth and clean. Many also give a weak bond unless the surfaces mate perfectly; they are not suitable for filling gaps in loose joints. Finally, they are made for glueing specific materials, so make sure you use the right adhesive for the job. Ask your retailer for his advice.

## BENCH HOOKS

The bench hook is a simple piece of equipment that hooks over the edge of a bench top to hold a piece of wood steady while you saw through it with a tenon saw. It also protects your bench from the saw. You can make your own from scrap wood. Use a piece of 12 mm (½ in) thick plywood, roughly 230 × 150 mm (9× 6 in), and glue and screw a piece of 50 × 25 mm (2 × 1 in) softwood to each end as shown (left).

## CHAMFER

Chamfering means taking the sharp edge off a corner, primarily for safety, normally leaving it angled at 45 degrees. This is done using glasspaper, but the chamfer can be accentuated

to become a bevel for decorative effect. Here a plane is used to give a neater, more regular finish.

## CHISELS

Three types of chisel are in common use for general woodworking: the bevel-edged chisel, the firmer chisel, and the mortice chisel.

The bevel-edged chisel is best for fine work and joint making; its sloping edges allow it to reach into awkward corners. However, it is fairly delicate, so don't use it for heavy work. Instead, use a firmer chisel, which has a stronger rectangular-section blade, but even this will not stand the battering a chisel receives during morticing. This is a job for a mortice chisel, which has a very stocky blade, and a reinforced handle designed to take repeated heavy blows.

A set of firmer or bevel-edged chisels in 6 mm, 12 mm, and 25 mm (¼ in, ½ in, and 1 in) widths will cope with most jobs. If you need a mortice chisel, a 6 mm (¼ in) wide blade is probably of most use.

Once you have bought your chisels, learn to use them safely, and accurately. Before cutting a channel across a piece of timber (when making a joint, for example) mark out its width on the face and both edges of the timber with a try-square and a knife. Then, mark the depth with the aid of a marking gauge. These score lines are more accurate than pencil lines, but you can run over them in pencil to make them clearer. Place the wood in a vice and saw down each side of the channel with a tenon saw. Take the chisel and gradually remove one corner of the waste wood. Do this by holding the chisel blade in your left hand, so that it is angled upwards and then striking the handle with the palm of your right hand, or a mallet. When you reach the depth mark, turn the wood round and repeat the process to leave a triangular fillet of waste (left). Remove this to the correct depth with the chisel held level, finishing off by cleaning up in the corners (bottom).

Another useful technique is called paring – removing waste from an edge (above). Hold the chisel vertically, guiding its blade between the fingers of your left hand, and bear down on the handle with your right. Keep your right shoulder over the handle to apply plenty of pressure.

Of course, it all takes practice, but there are a few points to remember if the job doesn't go as it should. Keep chisels razor sharp, and look after them. Don't use them to open tins of paint, and if you need to strike the handle with something other than your hand, use a mallet if the chisel handle is wood. Don't try to take off too much wood in one go, and for safety's sake, keep your body (and those of anybody else) – hands, arms and all – behind the cutting edge at all times.

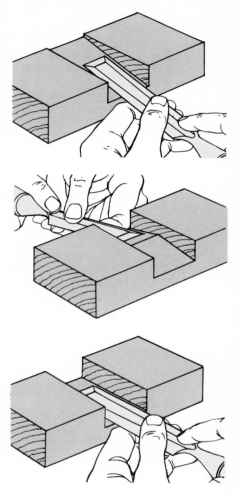

## COUNTERSINKING

Countersinking is setting a screwhead into the wood so that it finishes flush with the surface. Most woodscrews are for countersinking, having flat heads that flare out from the shank. For neat results, cut a recess for the head with a conical countersink rose drill bit (above right). Place

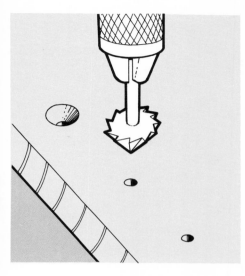

the point of the bit into the screw's clearance hole and operate the drill until the desired depth of countersink is achieved.

## CRAMPS

Most woodworking adhesives will give a far stronger joint if a little pressure is applied while they set. This is the job for the cramp.

For relatively small jobs, use a G-cramp. This consists of a cast, G-shaped frame with a fixed pad at one end and an adjustable screw pad at the other. For general work, keep two in your tool kit, each with a capacity of at least 150-200 mm (6-8 in). Simply tighten up the adjustable pad to clamp the workpiece, but remember to protect its surface with pieces of scrap wood (see page 110).

For bigger jobs use a sash cramp – a long bar with two heads that can be locked in various positions by metal pins. One head carries a screw

mechanism to apply the pressure, and provide final adjustment. Again, most jobs need two, but, unless you make a lot of furniture, hire them, rather than buy.

## DRILLING

Undoubtedly, an electric drill is very useful, but some people find it a handful, preferring to use a hand drill for .fine work. There are two main types. For small holes, you need a wheel brace and a set of twist bits between 1.5 mm (¹⁄₁₆ in) and 10 mm (³⁄₈ in) in diameter. Use a carpenter's hand brace for larger and/or deeper holes. Various bits are available for this, most in sizes up to about 50 mm (2 in).

Whatever tool you use, the principles of drilling are the same. Work with the drill at right-angles to the surface of the workpiece. If necessary, check this by holding a try-square against the work. Don't use too much force, as it is more likely to make the drill go askew. Do clamp the work firmly to a bench, or grip it in a vice. Withdraw the bit occasionally to clear the hole, keeping it turning in the same direction as when drilling. Avoid splintering as the drill breaks through the other side of the work by clamping a piece of scrap wood in the appropriate place, and drilling straight into it.

## MAN-MADE BOARDS

Don't think of man-made boards as cheap, inferior substitutes for natural timber. As sheet materials, they are superior, being stronger and less likely to warp.

Plywood consists of three or more

*A G-cramp holds a furniture repair while the adhesive sets.*

wood veneers glued together, the grain of each sheet running at right-angles to its neighbour to resist warping. It's strong, easily worked, but can be expensive if the outer veneers are in decorative hardwood.

Blockboard has a core of glued battens sandwiched between two or four outer veneers. It's less flexible than plywood, making it suitable for shelves, but tidying the edges can be difficult.

Hardboard (compressed wood fibre) is the cheapest man-made board. However, it isn't strong, and

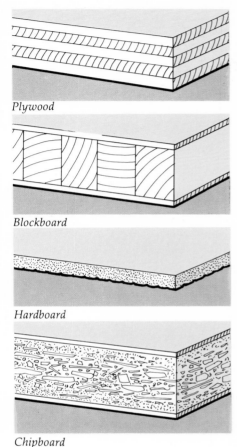

*Plywood*

*Blockboard*

*Hardboard*

*Chipboard*

## MORTICING

Morticing is a method of cutting a rectangular hole with a chisel. If the hole passes right through the workpiece, it is called a through mortice; if it doesn't, it is called a stopped mortice. In either case, the method of cutting it out is the same.

Mark the width of the mortice along the grain with a marking gauge, using a try-square and knife to mark the ends. To cut the mortice you need a chisel – preferably a mortice chisel – the same width as the hole, and a mallet. Position the chisel at one end of the mortice with its bevel facing in towards the middle. Then, hit it sharply with the mallet to drive it about 3 mm (⅛ in) into the wood. Pull it out, move it about 3 mm (⅛ in) along towards the mortice centre, and strike it again. Continue in this way until you reach the middle of the mortice, and repeat the process from the other end, reducing the surface of the waste wood to a series of chips. These can be levered out quite easily, allowing you to chop up and remove the next layer of waste.

For a stopped mortice, simply carry on until the hole is deep enough. Then, clean out the corners with a bevel-edged chisel. For a through mortice, it is better to stop halfway, turn the work over, and cut a second mortice to join up with the first. In this way, any splintering caused as the chisel finally breaks through will be hidden away in the centre of the wood. Obviously, accurate marking out is essential if this is to work.

Morticing with a chisel is a slow process, but there is a quicker

needs the support of a sturdy framework.

Finally, there is chipboard: a mixture of woodchips and glue pressed into a sheet, and sometimes finished with a decorative veneer. Relatively inexpensive, it is widely used for shelves and furniture. Unfortunately, it is difficult to work, very heavy, and does not take screws at all well.

111

*Position the chisel with the bevel facing towards the middle of the mortice.*

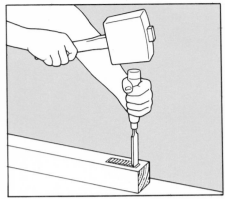

*When you reach the middle of the mortice, repeat from the other end.*

method worth trying. First, remove the bulk of the waste by drilling a series of holes as close to each other as possible. Finally, chisel out the timber in between.

## NAILS

Nails offer a quick and efficient way of strengthening a variety of joints. However, you must choose the right nail for the job, and use it properly. You don't just bang it into anything.

One of the most useful nails for general rough carpentry is the round wire nail. Available in sizes ranging from 20-150 mm (¾-6 in), it gives a strong, if not very neat, fixing. It can split the wood very easily, though.

To prevent splitting, use oval wire nails, also known as oval brads, driving them in with their long axes running with the grain to ease the wood fibres gently apart. Their other advantage is that their heads can be punched below the surface of the wood and covered with stopping, making them a good choice where

looks matter. Sizes range from 12 mm (½ in) to 150 mm (6 in).

Panel pins are for lightweight work, primarily fixing sheet materials such as plywood to a supporting timber framework. Therefore, the choice of size is limited to between 12 and 50 mm (½ and 2 in). Do not use them on hardboard, though. Here, a special type of pin, called a hardboard nail, is preferable. Another variation on the panel pin, worth remembering, is the veneer pin. This is very thin and is used to secure veneers and delicate timber mouldings.

Finally, there is the masonry nail – a specially hardened nail capable of making a rough, reasonably strong fixing in soft masonry and concrete. There are two main types: those with normal round shanks, and those with twisted shanks that are square in section. The latter should give a better grip, but both are quite brittle, so use them with care and wear safety goggles.

112

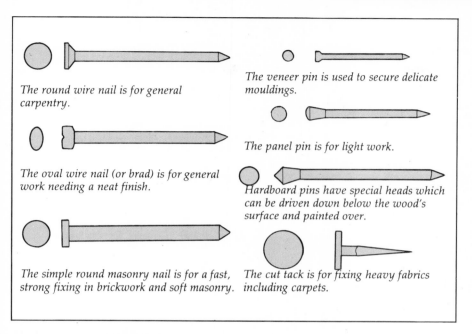

*The round wire nail is for general carpentry.*

*The oval wire nail (or brad) is for general work needing a neat finish.*

*The simple round masonry nail is for a fast, strong fixing in brickwork and soft masonry.*

*The veneer pin is used to secure delicate mouldings.*

*The panel pin is for light work.*

*Hardboard pins have special heads which can be driven down below the wood's surface and painted over.*

*The cut tack is for fixing heavy fabrics including carpets.*

## NAILING TECHNIQUES

The first thing you must learn is how to drive a nail in straight. Hold the point of the nail in place and gently tap it to set it in the wood – small pins can be held by pushing them through a piece of card. Assuming the nail has started straight, it should go in straight when you begin driving it more firmly with the hammer. If it doesn't, check that you are using the right size hammer – big nails need big hammers; small nails need small hammers. The idea is to avoid using undue force. Merely swinging the hammer in an arc from your wrist should be enough, and gives more control. If, in spite of everything, the hammer skips off the nail, clean its face by rubbing it over a sheet of glasspaper.

Often, when making joints, simple nailing is sufficient, provided the nail passes through the thinner of the two pieces to leave most of its length in the thicker piece. However, there is a risk that the nails will pull out if the joint is put under strain. To prevent this, either use nails long enough to pass through both pieces and hammer over their points to lock them in place (clench nailing), or drive the nails in at opposing angles (skew nailing).

## PLANES & PLANING

Unless you are serious about carpentry, it's really not worth buying more than one plane, and the best all-purpose type is a jack plane between 355 and 380 mm (14 and 15 in) long. Later, if you should decide to get a

113

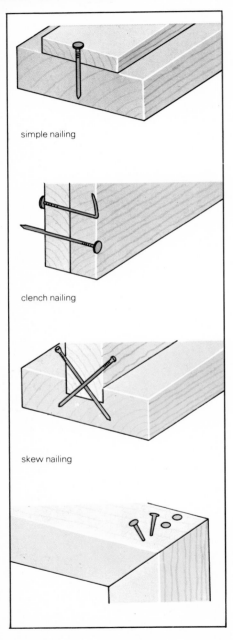

simple nailing

clench nailing

skew nailing

second plane, choose a 200-250 mm (8-10 in) smoothing plane, which will improve the finish left by the jack plane.

Before using a plane, you must ensure that it is set correctly. There are two basic controls for this: the knurled wheel behind the blade assembly, and the lever at the top. The wheel controls the amount of blade protruding below the sole; the lever lets you tilt the blade from side to side to set its cutting edge parallel with the sole. Check both settings by turning the plane upside down, pointing it towards a light or window, and sighting along the sole. A little practice is needed to judge the depth of cut correctly, so start with the blade fully retracted, and progressively lower it. Try it out at each stage, until the plane gives a clean, smooth, continuous shaving. Don't make the cut any thicker to speed up the work; you will get poor results as the blade digs in and judders across the surface.

Once the plane is set, grip the workpiece firmly in a vice, making sure that it is level, and begin planing by taking a shaving from the entire length of the wood in a single stroke – on wide boards you will find this easier if you hold the plane slightly askew in relation to the board's edge. Aim to keep the sole of the plane parallel with the floor at all times, without rocking it.

When planing a long piece of timber, try simply walking forwards, holding the plane level at your side. On shorter pieces, where it is only sensible to stand still, position yourself at the side of the work, and vary

## SANDING

To sand a piece of timber smooth, wrap the abrasive paper round a cork sanding block so it presents a flat surface to the work, and rub it gently back and forth along the line of the grain. Don't work it across the grain or it will leave scratches that may be difficult to remove. The one exception to this rule is endgrain, where it is best to work the abrasive over the surface with a circular scrubbing action.

The choice of abrasive is also important. Start with a coarse grade, and having made the workpiece as smooth as you can with that, switch to a medium grade. Finally, use a fine grade to achieve the desired finish.

Unfortunately, as soon as you apply paint or varnish to the sanded surface, it will become rough again. This is because some of the wood fibres in the surface absorb moisture from the finish and swell. Before applying the finish, therefore, wipe over the surface with a moist cloth, leave it for a few minutes, and sand it smooth again while still damp. This removes most of the fibres that are likely to swell.

## SAWS & SAWING

Most small sawing jobs are best tackled with a tenon saw. This gives a fairly fine, and therefore accurate, cut. Unlike some saws, it is equally at home cutting across the grain as along it.

The first technique to master is sawing across the grain. Carefully mark a cutting line right round the timber, using a knife and try-square. A knife mark is more accurate than a

the amount of downward pressure you apply as the plane moves past you. At the beginning of each cut, most of the pressure should be on the front of the plane; by the time you reach the end of the cut, the pressure should have been transferred to the back.

Having removed four or five shavings, check that the edge is straight by holding it up to a window and laying a straight edge along it. Any low spots will show as chinks of light. Check that the edge is square in the same way, using a try-square.

Planing across the end grain (above) is rather different. Here, if you take off the waste in a single stroke, the far edge of the wood will splinter. To prevent this, set the plane to give a very fine cut, and remove the waste by working in from both ends towards the centre of the wood. Alternatively, clamp a piece of scrap wood against the far edge of the workpiece, and run the plane over both workpiece and scrap. The scrap wood should hold the vulnerable far edge together.

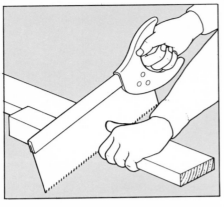

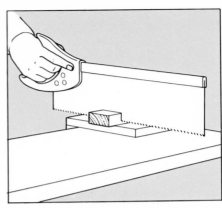

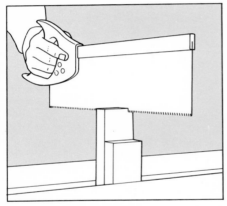

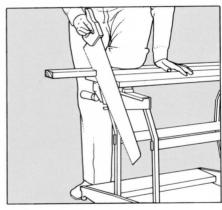

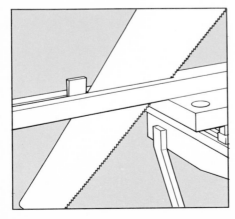

*Top left: Begin the cut by drawing the saw over the far edge of the wood, guiding the blade with your thumb.*

*Top right: Gradually reduce the saw's angle until level, and continue sawing.*

*Centre left: When sawing along the grain of the wood, grip the work in a vice. Using a backing piece of scrap wood will help to reduce vibration.*

*Above: With a cross-cut saw, keep the blade at 60 degrees throughout.*

*Left: If the saw sticks when sawing along the grain, open up the cut with scrap timber fillets.*

pencil line, and it also cuts through the surface fibres of the wood, helping to give a cleaner finish. If you find the knife lines difficult to see, run over them in pencil.

Hold the wood tight against the end stop of a bench hook with your left hand (top left). Position the saw blade on the waste side of the cut line, where it turns the far edge, pointing it downwards slightly to do this. Then, guiding the blade with your thumb, draw the saw backwards two or three times.

When you have produced a shallow notch in the wood, change your grip so that your fingers are out of harm's way. Work the saw back and forth, concentrating your effort on the forward strokes – these are the cutting strokes – to deepen the cut. Gradually reduce the angle of the saw, extending the cut across the face of the timber, until it is perfectly level. Keeping it level, continue sawing right through the wood so that you just graze the bench hook with the last few strokes.

While you are working, check that the saw is following the cut line. If it is not, make sure you are holding it with your forefinger pointing along the blade to stop it waving about, and you are standing so that your elbow is clear of your body when your arm comes back. You should also have a good view of both saw and cut line. Lastly, let the saw do the work – don't force it.

Cuts along the grain are tackled in much the same way; the only difference is that you must grip the work in a vice (centre left). Keep it as low in the vice as possible to reduce

vibration. If the workpiece is too long to allow this, back it with a piece of scrap wood, and clamp the two together to give extra stiffness.

For larger work, use a cross-cut saw. This is longer, and gives a coarser cut, but the sawing technique is only slightly different. Rest the workpiece on a saw-horse or portable vice with its cut line overhanging the end; hold it down with your knee. Start the cut in the same way as with a tenon saw, but steady the blade with your thumb. When you begin sawing in earnest, keep the saw at an angle, slowing down and steadying the waste with your left hand just before you saw right through.

You can saw along the grain in the same way, but, because cross-cut saws are not really designed for this job, they tend to jam as the cut progresses. To prevent this, wedge the cut open at intervals with thin scraps of wood or card.

## SCREWS
In most situations, screws give stronger fixings than nails. The most widely used types are shown overleaf.

The countersunk (see Countersinking, page 108) woodscrew could be considered a general-purpose screw, but the round-headed screw is more specialized. Although sometimes used to secure sheet materials, the main job of the latter is to retain metal fittings that do not have countersunk holes. Where these are provided, the raised-head screw is generally used instead.

Finally, there are screws with a cross-shaped recess in the head

*Countersunk head. For general carpentry and joinery.*

*Roundhead. For fixing sheet material too thin to be countersunk.*

*Raised countersunk head. For use with ironmongery and screwcups.*

*Dome head. For fixing mirrors and plastic panels.*

*Other drive methods. Phillips, Posidriv and Supadriv heads.*

## SCREWING

Although it is fairly obvious how you drive home a screw, there a few little tricks worth knowing.

Don't try to drive a screw into virgin wood. Drill a clearance hole, large enough to take the unthreaded screw shank, through the piece you want to fix, widening the mouth with a countersunk bit if necessary. Then, drill a pilot hole, smaller in diameter than the threaded portion of the screw, in the piece to which you want to make the fixing.

With slotted screws, the screwdriver's tip width must match the screw head as closely as possible. An undersize tip will chew up the slot; an oversize one will scratch the workpiece. The length of the blade should also be considered. Long blades give more turning power than short blades.

## SHARPENING

If you want to work quickly and efficiently, producing consistently good results, your tools must be sharp. Drill and saw sharpening is best left

instead of the normal slot. This stops the screwdriver slipping. These are now very common, and are to be found matching most of the standard slotted screw designs. There are different versions, however – Pozidriv, Supadriv, and the now-defunct Phillips head patterns are the most common – each of which, in theory at least, needs a slightly different screwdriver.

Most come in lengths ranging from 9-152 mm (⅜-6 in) and in gauge numbers 4 to 14 – the higher the number the thicker the screw.

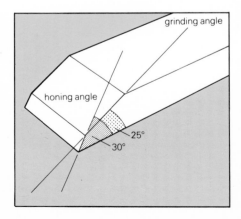

to experts, but you can sharpen chisels and plane irons yourself. You need some light machine oil, and an oil stone.

When sharpening a chisel, liberally coat the surface of the stone with oil. Hold the chisel blade in both hands at 30 degrees (below) – the honing angle – and work it over the stone until a fine burr of metal appears behind the cutting edge. Take care not to rock the chisel while doing this. If you find this difficult, buy a honing guide to steady the blade at exactly the right angle. Stroke off the burr, holding the back of the chisel blade flat against the stone, and the tool is ready for use.

Plane blades are tackled in much the same way; the only difference is that not all planes have straight cutting edges. Smoothing plane blades have rounded corners to stop them digging in, and jack plane blades have a pronounced overall curve designed to remove waste more quickly.

## WOOD

There are two basic classes of timber: softwood, and hardwood. Contrary to what might seem common sense, this classification has nothing to do with the wood's physical hardness – though the majority of hardwoods are harder than the majority of softwoods. The distinction is that hardwoods come from deciduous trees, while softwoods come from conifers.

Of the two, hardwoods are generally superior, in that they are stronger, more atrractive, and can be more accurately worked. However, they can be extremely expensive, and

so are rarely seen except as decorative veneers.

The sort of timber you are most likely to come across is therefore softwood – usually pine, but almost invariably sold simply as 'softwood'. It's not the sort of wood you would use for top quality furniture, but it is adequate for most purposes. And it is relatively inexpensive.

Softwood comes in a range of standard sections based on multiples of the 'metric inch' (25 mm), and in standard lengths based on multiples of the 'metric foot' (300 mm). Therefore, you must be careful when buying; if you have worked out what you need in imperial measurements, you will get less than you bargained for. It is best to work in metric units.

Even so, you may have problems with the section sizes. Timber may be sold rough sawn or ready planed, yet all dimensions specified by the retailer refer to the rough sawn size. If you buy wood that has been planed all round (PAR), it will be smaller all round than its nominal size suggests, because it started out as a rough sawn size. In fact, you can reckon on losing up to 3 mm (⅛ in) per side, so remember to allow for this when making calculations.

When buying, it is also worth checking on the quality of the timber offered. You have to expect, and accept, some defects, which is why it is wise to order a little more wood than you need – you can then cut the defects out. However, if the wood contains a lot of loose, dried out, dead knots; if it contains a long split, or if it is seriously twisted along its length, don't take it.

# GLOSSARY

**Aggregate** Material that, when mixed with cement and water, makes mortars, concrete and render.

**Air-brick** Perforated brick included in a wall to aid ventilation.

**Ampere (amp; A)** Unit of electric current expressing volume of flow.

**Beading** Small timber or plastic moulding used as decoration.

**Bevel** Angled edge.

**Blinding** Spreading a smooth, level layer of sand over compacted hardcore before laying concrete.

**Bolster chisel** A cold chisel with a blade about 100 mm (4 in) wide, used with club hammer for cutting bricks, blocks, paving slabs, etc.

**Bond** The way in which successive courses of bricks are laid to ensure that vertical joints are normally staggered.

**Brushing out** Spreading out paint to an even thickness on surface.

**Cable** Used for circuit wiring.

**Cartridge fuse** Small fusé used in plugs and fused connectors: 13 amp (brown) for appliances with load of 750W and over; 3 amp (red) for appliances and lamp with less than 750W.

**Cavity wall** A wall consisting of outer and inner 'leaves' separated by a gap or cavity about 50 mm (2 in) wide.

**Cement** Fine powder, made from burnt limestone and clay, which hardens when mixed with water. The 'glue' in concrete, mortar and render.

**Chase or chasing** A channel or groove cut out to receive a pipe or wiring, for example.

**Circuit breaker** Switch that automatically breaks contact in the event of overloading or a short circuit. Miniature circuit breaker (MCB) is alternative to a fuse.

**Cladding** Decorative timber (or PVC) boards, usually interlocking, for exterior house walls.

**Club hammer** Hammer with an oblong head, used with bolster and other cold chisels.

**Consumer unit** Consumer's fuse board, usually with an on/off switch.

**Coping** Topmost course of brick, block or stone wall; designed to throw off or resist penetration by moisture and so protect the wall as a whole.

**Course** A horizontal layer of bricks.

**Crowsfoot spanner** For tightening back nuts on taps.

**Current** Movement or flow of electricity, expressed in amps.

**Damp-proof course (DPC)** A water-impermeable layer built into a wall to bar the upward movement of ground moisture. A DPC is commonly laid over the second brick course above ground level; it is made of bituminous felt; slate and other materials are also used.

**Dormer** Vertical window built into the slope of a pitched roof.

**Dowel** Headless, cylinder-shaped peg used (with glue) to join pieces of wood; available in standard diameters of 3-50 mm (⅛-2 in).

**Earth** Conductor enabling electricity to pass into the earth.

**Eaves** Bottom edge of a pitched roof overhanging the walls.

**Efflorescence** A harmless, fluffy, white deposit on brickwork, caused by water-soluble salts being drawn to the surface.

**Fascia board** Timber planking, hung on edge from the end of rafters at the eaves, to which gutter is fixed.

**Flashing** Lead, zinc or felt waterproofing of the angle made by abutting vertical and pitched or horizontal surfaces on a roof.

**Flaunching** Sloping mortar fillet around chimney pots or behind firebacks.

**Flex** Used for connecting up electrical appliances.

**Frog** The depression (often V-section) in the surface of a standard brick.

**Fuse** Intentionally weak link in a circuit, designed to fail or break contact if system is overloaded.

**Fused connection unit** Used on a ring circuit or spur to connect an appliance without using a plug.

**Gable** House wall supporting ends of a pitched roof.

**Galvanized** When steel is galvanized, it has been coated with zinc to prevent rust.

**Gauge rod** A straight piece of timber, up to 1.5 m (5 ft) long and 50-75 mm (2-3 in) wide, with marks every 75 mm (the height of a brick plus its mortar bed). Used to ensure the courses of a brick wall rise evenly.

**Gauge, marking** Tool for scoring a line parallel to a face or edge of timber. A mortice gauge scores two parallel lines a variable distance apart.

**Gland** Sealing ring around the stem of tap, valve, and other fittings to prevent leaks.

**Gravity circulation** Circulation of water in a system that depends on the property of hot water to rise above cold. Heat is applied at a low point in the circuit.

**Grout** Filler used between ceramic tiles and mosaics.

**Gully** Opening to a drainage system.

**Hawk** Square plywood or metal plate on short handle for holding small quantity of mortar close to wall in patching and pointing work.

**Header** A brick laid with its end faces parallel with the line of the wall.

**Immersion heater** Metal-sheathed electrical element inserted into hot-water cylinder or tank to heat the water.

**Inspection chamber** Often called a manhole; a point of access to an underground drainage system.

**Insulator** Non-conducting material used for isolating a conductor.

**Joint, capillary** Method of joining copper pipe in which, when heat is applied, solder is conducted by capillary action between the pipe and a special fitting.

**Joist** Timber or steel beam supporting a floor or ceiling.

**Key** To roughen a surface so that another material can adhere to it.

**Knotting** Shellac-based solution for sealing knots in wood.

**Lagging** Protection of water tanks and pipes by insulation wrapping.

**Laying off** Final, light brush strokes in painting to give a perfectly smooth surface.

**Load-bearing wall** Wall carrying the weight of a superstructure such as a roof or second storey.

**Loop-in method** Connects up a lighting circuit to each ceiling rose in turn.

**Making good** Getting rid of surface defects before decorating.

**Medium** In paint, the liquid vehicle, such as oil or water, in which the pigment is suspended.

**Mortar** General term for various mixtures of sand and cement and/or lime used for binding bricks, blocks, etc., together.

**Moulding** Decorative, shaped strip or edge of wood or plaster.

**Noggin** Horizontal member of the timber framework of a partition wall.

**Nominal size** Standard 'as-sawn' dimensions of a piece of timber before being planed down.

**Ohm** Unit of electrical resistance (the resistance of wiring to passage of electricity).

**Pantile** High-profiled roof tile that interlocks with its neighbours on either side.

**PAR** Planed all round: machine-smoothed timber in which width and depth are commonly 3 mm (⅛ in) less than the nominal size.

**Parquet** Hardwood flooring blocks laid in symmetrical patterns.

**Partition** Non-load-bearing internal wall.

**Pebbledash** An external wall surface made of fine gravel thrown on to soft mortar.

**Perpend** A vertical mortar joint.

**Pier** Bonded-in reinforcement for brick or block wall to increase its vertical stability.

**Pigment** Finely ground substance that provides the colour in paint.

**Pilaster block** In screen-block walls, a purpose-made pier with a groove on one or more sides into which screen blocks are slotted.

**Plane, block** Metal plane suitable for small work and end-grain trimming.

**Plane, moulding** Small, narrow-bladed plane for forming shaped edges to timber.

**Plane, plough** Plane for cutting a groove or rebate.

**Plane, shoulder** Narrow-bladed plane for cleaning up the surfaces of joint shoulders, mortices and tenons.

**Pointing** A decorative finish to mortar joints.

**Primer** The first coat of paint on a surface. Different types are used for different surfaces (wood, steel, non-ferrous metals, and so on) to provide good protection and achieve maximum adhesion.

**PTFE** Tape or paste waterproofing compound containing polytetrafluorethylene used for sealing joints in pipes and other fittings.

**PVA** Polyvinyl acetate, the basis of various types of adhesives and paints.

**Radial circuit** System in which circuit cables radiate from a consumer unit.

**Rafter** One of the beams forming the framework of a pitched roof.

**Rail** (1) Horizontal timber of a door. (2) Horizontal timber from which vertical boards of a fence or pales of a gate are hung.

**Render** Mortar applied as a protective and decorative screed to external brick or block walls. Typically a 1:4 mix of cement and sharp and soft sand.

**Ridge** Junction of two slopes at top of a pitched roof.

**Ridge board** Timber board to which upper ends of rafters are fixed.

**Ridge tile** Square- or round-profile tile that covers the ridge.

**Ring circuit** System arranged in form of a ring starting from and returning to the same circuit fuse of circuit-breakers.

**Rising main** Pipe that brings water into house from the Water Board's system.

**Scribing** Marking a cutting line, usually with a knife or sharp instrument.

**Short circuit** Connection (usually accidental) between two sides of a circuit.

**Size** Thinned adhesive used to seal a surface before hanging wallcovering.

**Slater's ripper** Tool for cutting through nails when damaged slates are replaced.

**Sliding bevel** Essentially a try square with a movable blade pivoted about one end of the stock. For marking angles other than right angles.

**Soffit board** Horizontal timber planking hung between fascia board and wall.

**Sole plate** Horizontal member of partition framework, fixed to floor.

**Spotboard** Flat board, about 1 m (3 ft 3 in) square, for mixing mortar or bringing it close to work. Usually made of plywood supported by battens.

**Spur** Branch cable attached to a ring circuit.

**Spur post** Concrete or timber reinforcement for lower portion of fence post.

**Stile** Vertical member of a gate, door, or window-frame.

**Stop-cock** Hand-operated on/off valve permitting water flow in only one direction.

**Stud** Vertical member of the timber framework of a partition wall.

**Terminal** That part of an appliance, socket, plug or switch to which electrical conductors are fixed.

**Tile gauge** Straight piece of timber marked with tile and tile-and-a-half widths to ensure correct bond when tiling.

**Tiler's spike** Sharp-pointed tool for scoring through the glaze of ceramic tiles prior to cutting them.

**Trap** Water-filled fitting below a sink, bath, gully or WC to prevent smells rising from drains.

**Undercoat** Paint applied after the primer to provide a neutral base for the top coat(s).

**Valley** Internal angle formed by junction of two pitches.

**Valve, ball** Used to control level of water in a cistern.

**Valve, bleed** Used, with a key, to evacuate air trapped in a central-heating system.

**Valve, gate** Hand-operated on/off valve permitting water to flow in either direction.

**Valve, safety** Operated by pressure; opens when pressure exceeds a pre-selected level.

**Volt (V)** Unit of the pressure that causes an electric current to flow in a circuit.

**Wall plate** Timber beam, laid on top of brick or block wall, to which ends of joists or rafters are fixed.

**Watt (W)** Unit of power: 1 watt equals the work represented by a current of 1 amp under a pressure of 1 volt. The kilowatt (kW) is a unit equal to 1,000 watts; it is the unit by which the power (and electrical consumption) of most domestic electrical appliances is defined.

# INDEX

PDO 83-274